Intimations of Reality

THE MENDENHALL LECTURES
1983

Intimations of Reality
Critical Realism in Science and Religion

BY

ARTHUR PEACOCKE

PUBLISHED FOR
DePauw University
Greencastle, Indiana
BY
University of Notre Dame Press
Notre Dame, Indiana

Copyright © 1984 by
University of Notre Dame Press
Notre Dame, Indiana 46556

Library of Congress Cataloging in Publication Data

Peacocke, A. R. (Arthur Robert)
  Intimations of reality.

  "The Mendenhall lectures, 1983."
  Bibliography: p.
  1. Science—Philosophy. 2. Religion and science—
1946-   . I. Title. II. Title: Mendenhall lectures.
Q175.P347 1984   501   84-40357
ISBN 0-268-01155-9
ISBN 0-268-01156-7 (pbk.)

Manufactured in the United States of America

Contents

Acknowledgments

The preparation of these lectures was greatly assisted by the willingness of Dr. Janet Martin Soskice of Somerville College, Oxford, to make available to me her 1982 Oxford University D.Phil. thesis on "The Use of Metaphor as a Conceptual Vehicle of Religious Language", and by Professor Ernan McMullin, of the University of Notre Dame, providing me with a copy of his unpublished paper on "The Case of Scientific Realism." I am grateful to these authors for allowing me to quote from their work and for the helpful discussions I had with them. I am particularly indebted to Dr. Jean van Altena for her expert editorial advice and for the enrichment of the text through her theological and musical insight.

The occasion of the delivery of these 1983 Mendenhall Lectures at DePauw University was made pleasurable by the warm hospitality of the President and his colleagues. I am very glad they gave me that opportunity of sharing my thoughts with them.

Arthur Peacocke
April 1984

Foreword

When Arthur R. Peacocke, Dean of Clare College, Cambridge University, consented to present the Mendenhall Lectures at DePauw University on October 25-26, 1983, he complemented a distinguished group of scholars who had similarly opened new vistas and depths of religious thought and knowledge to listeners on the campus.

The Mendenhall Lectureship was established in 1905 through a bequest by Marmaduke H. Mendenhall, minister of the North Indiana Conference of the Methodist Episcopal Church, and member of the Board of Trustees of DePauw University. The will specified that income from the fund was to be used "for the support of an annual lectureship, the design of which shall be the exhibition of the proofs, from all sources, of the Divine Origin, inspiration, and authority of the Holy Scriptures." The intentions of the Reverend Mendenhall have been fulfilled over the years by such eminent speakers as Peter Bertocci, L. Harold DeWolf, Neal F. Fisher, Langdon Gilkey, Rollo May, J. Robert Nelson, Albert Outler, Ralph W. Sockman, Cynthia Wedel, and Colin Williams.

The 1983 Mendenhall Lectures and the programs surrounding them were brought to focus by Dr. Peacocke's concern with the interaction between his two teaching disciplines — theology and science. The lectureship, spanning two days, was highlighted by the awarding of honorary degrees to the speaker and four other prominent servants of the church — the Reverend B. Willis Gierhart, Ms. Carolyn Marshall, Bishop Roy C. Nichols, and Bishop Federico J.

Pagura. Bishop Emeritus Ralph T. Alton assisted in presentation of the degrees.

Joining the students, faculty, and staff of the University
were three other designated groups of visitors participating
in satellite programs of the lectureship. Representatives of
twenty-six seminaries were on campus to present their in-
stitutions to prospective students from DePauw and other
state colleges, as well as to join in dialogue with Dr. Robert W. Lynn, Vice President for Religion, Lilly Endow-
ment, Inc. A clergy group shared in Dr. Peacocke's seminar, "Creation and Evolution," and members of the Indiana
Area Cabinet of the United Methodist Church in the Bishop's "Seminar on Human Rights."

Arthur Peacocke's two primary addresses, "Ways to the
Real World" and "God's Action in the Real World," constitute this book.

Richard F. Rosser
President
DePauw University

1

Ways to the Real World

"Realism"—the catchword of the early 1980s. All over the Western world, at least—and one senses from the reports a similar mood in Moscow—the hard-nosed realists have captured public support, and our leaders ply us with over-doses of so-called economic and military "realism." This has the effect of blinding us to the realities, on the one hand, of the deprived and distressed (who everywhere in the Western world are becoming relatively more numerous than before) and, on the other hand, of the simple moral enormity and crass *non*-realism of the mounting pile of nuclear weapons more than sufficient for overkill. That kind of so-called "realism" is certainly accounted a virtue today in the public forum. But, of course, as I have hinted, it is shot through with make-believe and illusion about the hard facts of life and death for the peoples of the world. Ordinary human beings, who are less captives of the media than the powers-that-be might wish, seek their own paths to reality. We are faced, as Solzhenitsyn reminded us, to our discomfort, in his 1983 Templeton Award address, with an extraordinary loss of nerve in the West consequent upon the breakdown of the Christian consensus on which our ethics and liberties were formerly founded. After in-itiating us as only he could—indeed, as only he had the right to do—into the unimaginable sufferings of the Rus-sian people through war from outside and persecution from within, he turned his piercing eye on the West:

> The West has yet to experience a communist inva-sion; religion remains free. But the West's own his-

torical evolution has been such that today it, too, is experiencing a drying up of religious consciousness. It, too, has witnessed racking schisms, bloody religious wars, and enmity, to say nothing of the tide of secularism which, from the late Middle Ages onward, has progressively inundated the West. This gradual sapping of strength from within is a threat to faith that is perhaps even more dangerous than any attempt to assault religion violently from without.

Unnoticeably, through decades of gradual erosion, the meaning of life in the West ceased to stand for anything more lofty than the pursuit of "happiness," a goal that has even been solemnly guaranteed by constitutions. The concepts of good and evil have been ridiculed for several centuries; banished from common use, they have been replaced by political or class considerations of short-lived value. It has become embarrassing to appeal to eternal concepts, embarrassing to state that evil makes its home in the individual human heart before it enters a political system. Yet it is not considered shameful to make daily concessions to an integral evil. Judging by the continuing landslide of concessions made before the eyes of our very own generation, the West is ineluctably slipping toward the abyss.[1]

This being the case — and those of us present at this address could not avoid its truth (we knew then what it must have been like to have heard Amos, or, to have been confronted, like David, by Nathan: "*Thou* art the man") — is it at all surprising that our Western societies today reveal an unprecedented and frenetic search for "reality" that generates a babble of conflicting voices asking "What's 'for real'?" In this supermarket, many delicately select according to their own preconceived notions or, make their own mix, as from a smorgasbord, according to their taste—from among the panaceas of Divine Light, Transcendental Meditation, 'Unification' religion, theosophy, punk rock, serial music, jogging, or aerobics. But, within this cacophony, two voices continue to ring out because they gain a universal audience—the older voice of religion and the younger one of science.

Ever since the emerging species of *homo sapiens* started burying its dead with ritual, mankind has displayed an awareness of the tragedy of the ephemeral, the reality and yet the inner unacceptability of the cycle of life and death, and has sought a transcendent meaning in another Reality for that brief flickering into self-consciousness which all its members experience. Thus the religious quest, the long search for meaning and significance, is one of the most characteristic features of all societies—and I do not exclude our own, for there are rooms waiting to be filled by God in the interior castle of every Western soul; if they remain empty and ungarnished, a plethora of new twentieth century devils rush in to fill them.

Today, just as universally, science is the common possession of and common factor pervading all cultures. It is a dominating force shaping the outlook of mankind everywhere, especially that of the young—even modifying the language and affecting the images that most readily come to mind; it simply cannot be ignored by anyone concerned with the plausibility of Christianity or any other religion.

The relationship between these two claimants on mankind's loyalty is probably the most fundamental challenge that faces the mind and spirit of human beings today. Most of us have been brought up to believe, consequent upon the so-called, but certainly blinkered, Enlightenment and in the aftermath of the nineteenth century Darwinian controversies, that as the star of science waxes that of religion must of course wane. We have been conned by the mythology of the "warfare," "conflict," and "struggle" between science and religion, especially Christian theology.[2] Since we are all realists now, we have to opt for one or the other. It was not always so, for the history of the relation between the natural sciences and Christian theology—certainly in my own national and ecclesiastical tradition—has shown more integrated and fruitful relationships, at least in the past. We will not linger over that history now, for only when we have examined how far science and religion live up to the claims made for them can we pursue further what kind of relationships are possible. Does science, does religion, tell us about a world that is real *to us*?

I. THE SCIENTIFIC ENTERPRISE

(a) *The current status of science.* There was a time, for a decade or so after the end of the Second World War, when scientists were assigned a role in society not unlike that of priests in medieval Europe. But there is no doubt that science now has a tarnished image, not least among many of the young. There has been in fact a long tradition of antiscientific attitudes in Western cultural life, mainly stemming from a profound dissatisfaction with scientific "explanations" that do not answer the questions that mankind actually poses.[3] A word, an ugly one, has even been coined for the imperialism of science in our intellectual and cultural life, "scientism," the attitude that says all our personal and social problems are "soluble" in the long run by science.

Even so, we all accept that, within the limits of human error, technology *works*, and, even if somewhat grudgingly, we still regard the natural sciences which feed technology (and this now very much includes the biological and medical sciences) as the paradigm of what constitutes reliable knowledge. The corollary of this is that other forms of enquiry are tacitly demoted relative to the sciences with respect to the status and reliability of the knowledge they engender. Or, from psychology through sociology and economics to the study of human behavior, they adopt the style and approach of the natural sciences, even to borrowing the debased vocabulary and syntax of computer jargon. Science allows prediction and control, and most people need little further argument that what it says is "true" and what it refers to is "real." So most laymen's, and many scientists', view of scientific concepts and mechanisms is that they are literal descriptions of the world, reproductions of objective reality, mainly on the basis that "science works." According to this view, called "naive realism," science really discovers, that is, un-covers, the hidden mechanisms of the world of nature and shows us what is *actually* there.

However, the world described by some areas of modern physics and astrophysics is a very strange one indeed, far removed from simple extrapolations from the world observable by our senses to the very small and the very large. It is intriguing, from among the concepts and terms used in science, to make a list graded from those that refer to entities that, in the ordinary sense, are generally thought "really to exist" to those whose ontological status is, to say the least, problematic. Here is one such possible list: the circulation of the blood, anthrax bacteria, proteins as chains of amino acids, water as H_2O, molecules, atoms, atomic nuclei, quasars, mass, baryons, energy, dilation of space and time, entropy, black holes, electron holes, antimatter, gravitational waves, spin, "charm," virtual particles, . . . phlogiston? caloric fluid? I have deliberately ended with concepts that are no longer current in science and have now been discarded from its repertoire. Such a list highlights one of the basic questions in the philosophy of science, namely

"To what do scientific terms refer, and what is their relation to observation?" To ask such questions is clearly to ask to what extent science describes the real world.

It has been said that the average scientist knows what he is doing about as much as the average centipede knows how it walks! Be that as it may, it is the analyses of scientific thinking and activity by philosophers and sociologists that have provided cogent insights into these questions. So to these we must turn if we wish to formulate our own judgment concerning the degree to which, or even the possibility that, science may be a way to the reality we wish to know and adjust to.

(b) *The "received view" (or "standard account") of the structure of scientific theories*, which held sway from the 1920s to the 1970s,[4] used the methods and tools of mathematical and philosophical logic to interpret the activity of science and to justify it as an essentially logical enterprise.[5] Scientific theories were to be axiomatized logically into three kinds of terms: logical and mathematical; theoretical; and observational. Theoretical terms are merely abbreviations for descriptions that involve only observational terms. "Correspondence rules" explicitly coordinate the theoretical terms. This initial form of this account of scientific theories underwent considerable development and refinement but remained based upon the presuppositions of naive realism, a universal scientific language, and the correspondence theory of truth. As Mary Hesse has recently recalled:

> These three assumptions between them constitute a picture of science and the world somewhat as follows: there is an external world which can in principle be exhaustively described in scientific language. The scientist, as both observer and language-user, can capture the external facts of the world in propositions

that are true if they correspond to the facts and false if they do not. Science is ideally a linguistic system in which true propositions are in one-to-one relation to facts, including facts that are not directly observed because they involve hidden entities or properties, or past events or far distant events. These hidden events are described in theories, and theories can be inferred from observation, that is, the hidden explanatory mechanism of the world can be discovered from what is open to observations. Man as scientist is regarded as standing apart from the world and able to experiment and theorize about it objectively and dispassionately.[6]

She goes on to say that "almost every assumption underlying this account has been subjected to damaging criticism." There is, for example, a great logical problem about the inference of theories from observations, a problem called the *under-determination of theory* by empirical data.[7] There are also problems about the "data," for all facts are "theory-laden." Moreover the coherence conditions that theories are supposed to satisfy have themselves been subject to change (e.g., "simplicity" takes many forms) or downright replacement (e.g., the categories of space, time, causality have been radically changed by twentieth-century physics). So no simple convergence to a unique truth actually occurs. Indeed most aspects of this standard, "received," view of scientific theories have been successfully attacked.

It was not surprising that the late 1960s and early 1970s saw the demise of this view, especially rapidly after Thomas Kuhn's *Structure of Scientific Revolutions* (1962) gave a new impetus to reconsidering the history of science. For his interpretation of that history as consisting of periods of "normal" science, in which widely accepted paradigms were employed, exemplified, and applied, punctuated by periods of abnormal science, or revolutions, in which these paradigms

were irreversibly changed, excluded any obvious possibility
of convergence of concepts concerning a particular aspect of
the natural world. Not surprisingly, therefore—

(c) *Socially-contextualized (Weltanschauung) views of scientific
theories,*[8] which had developed over a long period as alter-
natives to the received view, became dominant during the
1970s, partly because of the influence of Kuhn's book. They
were based on a growing conviction that the distinction between the way a scientific result was obtained and the way
it was presented and justified could not be maintained in the
light of the actual history of any scientific discovery. So
there was no area for the application of the logic of the
"received" view that was neatly quarantined from the influences of the social context in which scientists worked
and from their whole worldview. Science came to be seen
as a continuous social enterprise, and the rise and fall of
theories and the use and replacement of concepts as involving a complex of personal, social, intellectual, and cultural
interactions that often determined whether a theory was accepted or rejected. Theories are constructed, it was argued,
in terms of the prevailing "worldview" of the scientists involved: so to understand them one must understand the
relevant worldview. A new emphasis was therefore placed
on the history of science, especially the sociological factors
influencing its development. Thus a new area was opened
up for the application of the expanding enterprise of the
sociology of knowledge in general and of scientific knowledge in particular. However, it turns out that the "worldview" of the scientist is an exceedingly complex and elusive
entity—even more so when a *community* of scientists is
involved.

At this stage there came a parting of the ways between,
on the one hand, those who develop these socially-contextualized views of scientific theories in the *sociology of scien-*

tific knowledge, especially in its so-called "strong program," and those, on the other hand, who think such views have failed to reveal anything of significance about the structure of scientific theories and adopt a form of scientific *realism* that can, of course, no longer be "naive," in the light of these intensive debates of the last three decades.

(d) *The sociology of scientific knowledge* is a more recent development within the general sociology of science. For a long period sociologists of science confined themselves to a study of the part played by science in modern society.[9] Sociology said nothing about the form or content of scientific knowledge itself, because the conclusions of science were thought to be determined by the physical, and not the social, world.

However, this inhibition has been overcome and natural science (and technology) has become subject to the scrutiny that sociologists have long directed towards other human activities, particularly religious and political ones. The program has been summarized thus by one of its proponents:

> Scientific knowledge-claims are not assessed by means of invariant, universal criteria. . . . contrary to the standard view, it seems that scientific knowledge is not stable in meaning, not independent of social context and not certified by the application of generally agreed procedures of verification.[10]

Such proponents argue that the thesis of the underdetermination of scientific theories by the observational evidence at least allows, and no longer excludes, the possibility of social factors being evoked to explain theory acceptance in the scientific community. The idea of the theory-ladenness of observations also leaves the way open for sociologists to study the patterns of preferences among observations displayed by scientists relative to their theoretical predispositions. Then it is only a short step to the "strong program" of the late 1970s in the sociology of knowledge, including scientific knowledge.

According to David Bloor,[11] its tenets are: (1) *causality*— concerned with conditions that bring about belief or states of knowledge; (2) *impartiality*—with respect to truth/falsity, rationality/irrationality, success/failure of the (scientific) ideas under consideration; (3) *symmetry*—in its style of explanation, the same types of causes explaining, say, true and false beliefs; (4) *reflexivity*—its pattern of explanation would have to be applicable to sociology itself (thereby, sawing off the branch on which it is sitting?). The sociologist, in this approach, is concerned with scientific knowledge as a natural phenomenon. Perhaps the strongest expression of this strong program and its consequences is that given by Mulkay:

> Scientific knowledge . . . offers an account of the physical world which is mediated through available cultural resources; and these resources are in no way definitive. . . . The physical world could be analysed perfectly adequately by means of language and pre-suppositions quite different from those employed in the modern scientific community. *There is, therefore, nothing in the physical world which uniquely determines the conclusions of that community.* . . . There is no alternative but to regard the products of science as social constructions like all other cultural products. . . . One of the central claims of the revised view is that scientific assertions are socially created and not directly given by the physical world as was previously supposed.[12]

From this it would seem that the sociologists of scientific knowledge have firmly barred the way of science to reality and instead see science as a complex of propositions and ideas that constitute a purely social construct. If this strong program were to be regarded as successful and dominant in our view of the status of scientific theories, there would have to be a radical reassessment of any previously supposed implications of the purported content of scientific knowledge in its relation to the religious and theological enterprise and its claim to be a "way" to reality. *Both* would be social ideologies.

But the strong program is not without its critics, and the resurgence of qualified forms of scientific realism provide an impressive and equally "strong" alternative to the implicit relativism of this sociological viewpoint. Ernan McMullin has argued[13] that, even though science is a social product, there is a crucial difference between it and most other such products. In science, the social and personal influences on theory that are occasionally distortive can and are limited by the progressive use of the complex test-methods characteristic of science. A continuous filtering and sifting proceeds from (and sometimes even before) the moment of publication, and this testing gradually uncovers where the distortions, if any, are located, whereupon they are progressively eliminated.[14] In McMullin's view, the relativist critique of science by the sociologists has not weakened the realist claim of the natural sciences, their cognitive privilege on matters concerning knowledge of the *natural* world.

It is, moreover, a fact that scientists have proved progressively more and more successful in predicting and manipulating the physical world, and, increasingly, also the biological. Any explanation of this phenomenon involves a rationalistic affirmation that "there are certain general truths about what makes one theory likely to be better than another which the scientific community has discovered and on which it by and large acts"[15] — and that the contemporary scientists' belief system contains more truth than that of their predecessors. Not *all* truth, just *more* — even if this "more" is only a miniscule increase, it is enough to ensure growth in the scientists' ability to predict and control. This fact of "progress," so defined, is set aside by the proponents of the strong program who see merely change, but not genuine progress, in the scientific enterprise. But appeals to changes in beliefs of scientists can explain such progress only if it is shown that those beliefs are true, or increasingly so, in some agreed sense, and this implies a rationalistic stance in assessing change. Furthermore, although, as Newton-Smith argues,[16] underlying the strong program is a view of the purely *social* causation of beliefs in the individual, no such causal laws linking the social and the cognitive have yet appeared.

The empirical sociological analyses of scientific knowledge cannot be lightly set aside. However, such work in relation to the concerns of this lecture—namely the extent to which science is a "way to reality"—cannot be taken to have the antirealist, antirationalist import that the proponents of the strong program sometimes seem to suggest. We must now turn to the development of, and arguments for, a more realist and rationalist assessment of science.

(e) *Scientific realism.* By 1969, these socially contextualized analyses were coming under increasingly heavy attack. According to Suppe, writing in 1977,[17] the philosophy of science had to become concerned with science as it is actually practiced—and a central and characteristic activity of science is the use of reason in propounding and developing theories and in evaluating them. So close attention began to be paid to actual scientific practice, both historical and contemporary.

Since 1977, the debate concerning scientific realism has intensified; indeed the revival of such a realism after decades of positivism is one of the most remarkable features of current analytical philosophy. Scientific realism is so called because it makes a proposal in regard to science, as such, not because it is "scientific" in any other sense. Indeed, it is basically a philosophical position. It must be made clear that no one wishes to go back to the "naive" realism that characterized the understanding of scientific language right up to the end of the nineteenth century. The revolution in physics in the first few decades of this century had already rendered it untenable and had generated the exceptional activity in the philosophy of science that has characterized the twentieth century. What might be a defensible, nonnaive scientific realism today, several decades since the revolution in physics? No one would want to be taken as attributing final truth to today's scientific theories—the history of science itself makes that impossible. Nor would one want to be appearing to give general approval to all the entities postulated by theories of the past that, however long they persisted, are now discarded. So what are the essential features of a realist position?

This question is closely linked with the much vexed philosophical problem of the nature of "truth." Hilary Putnam begins a discussion of "What is mathematical truth?" with an overly linguistic formulation:

> A realist (with respect to a given theory or discourse) holds that (1) the sentences of that theory are true or false; and (2) that what makes them true or false is something external—that is to say, it is not (in general) our sense data, actual or potential, or the structure of our mind, or our language, etc.[18]

The formulation of Putnam, sometimes called "convergent realism," reduces to the argument: (1) terms in mature theories typically refer to putative entities; and (2) mature theories are typically approximately true. This formulation does not do justice to the history of scientific theories, and Wilfred Sellars, for example, directs his attention more to the entities postulated in theories rather than to the theories per se. He says that "to have good reason for holding a theory is *ipso facto* to have good reason for holding that the entities postulated by the theory exist,"[19] and this constitutes scientific realism. In the light of these proposals, the antirealist van Fraasen puts forward the following as "the correct statement of scientific realism": "Science aims to give us, in its theories, a literally true story of what the world is like; and acceptance of a scientific theory involves the belief that it is true."[20] Note that unlike the naive version, this statement[21] says only that it is the *aim* of science to tell a true story; and the second part of the statement can allow gradations in acceptance, and thus gradations in belief in the truth of a scientific theory. A judicious and, he argues, defensible formulation of scientific realism has been given by Ernan McMullin in terms which will be adopted here as expressing the essentials of this position:

> The basic claim made by scientific realism . . . is that the long-term success of a scientific theory gives reason to believe that something like the entities and structure postulated in the theory actually exist. There are four important qualifications built into this: (1) the theory must be a successful one over a significant period; (2) the explanatory success of the theory gives some reason, though not a conclusive warrant, to believe [it]; (3) what is believed is that the theoretical structures are *something like* the structures of the real; (4) no claim is made for a special, more basic, privileged, form of existence for the postulated entities.[22]

Basically, scientific realism is "a quite limited claim which purports to explain why certain ways of proceeding in science have worked out as well as they (contingently) did." As McMullin admits, the qualifications ("significant period," "some kind," "something like"), although vague, seem to be essential to a defensible scientific realism. Their vagueness is somewhat dispelled by consideration of the use of metaphor in science, to which we shall come later. In any case, he is able to mount a formidable case for scientific realism, based on the historical fact that in many parts of natural science (e.g., geology, cell biology, chemistry) there has been over the last two centuries a progressive and continuous discovery of hidden structures in the entities of the natural world, structures that account causally for the observed phenomena.

This does not deny that practicing scientists are instinctively aware of the extent and nature of the provisionality that is assigned to theories in their chosen fields of enquiry and to the models associated with them. This tacit awareness of provisionality is shared by the subcommunity of scientists in any particular field and is acquired by their common experience of working on the problems posed by that aspect of the natural world. In practice, working scientists, I would argue,[23] adopt a skeptical and qualified realism, according to which their theories and models are proposed and regarded as "candidates for reality."[24] Scientists *aim* to depict previously hidden or unknown structures and processes of the real world, and the terms in their theories and the features of their models are intended genuinely to refer to a real world. They have no illusions, however, about the permanence of their proposals and the massive qualifications required of any attribution of "truth" to them. Nevertheless, there is more often than not an increasing sense of confidence in the reality of reference and a recognition of success in explanation, even as understanding modifies and changes. (Most sciences do *not* undergo revolutions like the one in physics that has so dominated the thinking of philosophers of science.) This consensus of the community of working scientists cannot be lightly set aside, based as it is on the experience that the knowledge of causal entities so obtained actually *works* in prediction and control of the natural world and in design of new experiments.

It is, I surmise, an increasing awareness of this character of the shared scientific enterprise that has caused the swing back to a scientific realism that is now qualified, but not to an extent that would have satisfied the positivists. It is urged that scientific change, since it actually manifests an increasing ability to predict and control (the "success" of science), is most readily comprehensible in realist terms — that is, scientists are understanding better and better the structures and processes of the natural world.

Such a view, what I have elsewhere[25] called a "sceptical and qualified" realism, is not instrumentalism, for it still allows high-level theories to be true or false in the usual correspondence sense. Moreover, it accepts the discontinuities ("revolutions") in the history of some (not all) sciences, such as physics.

This last may seem a modest virtue, but the argument from the existence of revolutions in the history of science — that is, radical discontinuities at the theoretical level — has in fact posed the greatest threat to the position of the scientific realist. To put this threat in the form of questions: Why should we have any confidence in what present-day science might seem to tell us about some aspect of the basic structure of the universe when science has changed its mind so often about this basic structure in the past? Does not the history of science demonstrate that the "entities" that make up the theories explaining observable phenomena at one period are drastically replaced in later revolutions (think of the disappearance of phlogiston, caloric, the ether, etc., from our purview)?

This is the so-called incommensurability thesis, or the problem of "translation," to the effect that past terms cannot be equated in meaning or reference with any terms or expressions we now possess. As Kuhn put it, scientists with different paradigms inhabit "different worlds": "electron" as used, say, in 1900, referred to objects in "one world"; as used today, it refers to objects in a quite different "world." But, to take this example of the electron, scientists are committed, on the basis of past evidence and current experience, to "believing in" electrons—that is, they cannot organize their current observations without asserting that electrons exist. *What* they believe about electrons may well, and has in fact, undergone many changes, but it is electrons to which they still refer, by long social links that go back to the first occasions on which they were "discovered" and the referring term "electron" was introduced. So physicists are committed to "believing in" the existence of electrons but remain hesitant about saying what electrons "are" and are always open to new ways of thinking about them that will enhance the reliability of their predictions and render their understanding more comprehensive with respect to the range of phenomena to which it is relevant.

However, the confidence of physicists in the existence of electrons, their confidence that the postulated entity "electron" is real, depends on much more than this continuous historical reference in a continuous linguistic community. It is also based on current experiments that they can perform, either in repetition of the original introducing experiments or, as Ian Hacking has recently emphasized,[26] in the devising of new experiments, in which previously postulated entities are used as tools. Because of experimentation, the degree of attribution of reality to such postulated entities can change from doubt about their existence, through thinking that to postulate their existence affords successful explanation, to an assured confidence in their existence through knowing how to *use* them. As Hacking[27] puts it:

> Experimental work provides the strongest evidence
> for scientific realism. This is not because we test hy-

potheses about entities. It is because entities that in principle cannot be 'observed' are regularly manipulated to produce new phenomena and to investigate other aspects of nature. They are tools, instruments not for thinking but for doing. The philosopher's favourite theoretical entity is the electron. . . . The more we come to understand some of the causal powers of electrons, the more we can build devices that achieve well-understood effects in other parts of nature. By the time that we can use the electron to manipulate other parts of nature in a systematic way, the electron has ceased to be something hypothetical, something inferred. It has ceased to be theoretical and has become experimental. . . . The vast majority of experimental physicists are realists about some theoretical entities, namely the ones they *use*. I claim that they cannot help being so. Many are also, no doubt, realists about theories too, but that is less central to their concerns. (p.262) . . . Electrons are no longer ways of organizing our thoughts or saving the phenomena that have been observed. They are ways of creating phenomena in some other domain of nature. Electrons are tools. (p.263) . . . *We are completely convinced of the reality of electrons when we regularly set out to build — and often enough succeed in building — new kinds of device that use various well-understood causal properties of electrons to interfere in other more hypothetical parts of nature.* (p.265)

This may be called the experimental argument for realism: it is a realism about *entities*, whose existence is affirmed by discerning causal lines, rather than a realism about *theories*, which can be very different and certainly more cautious and agnostic than the other. Realism about entities, Hacking argues, arises from what we can do at present. As he forcibly expresses it:

There are surely innumerable entities and processes that humans will never know about. Perhaps there are many that in principle we can never know about. Reality is bigger than us. The best kinds of evidence for the reality of a postulated or inferred entity is that we can begin to measure it or otherwise understand its causal powers. The best evidence, in turn, that we have this kind of understanding is that we can set out, from scratch, to build machines that will work fairly reliably, taking advantage of this or that causal nexus. Hence, engineering, not theorizing, is the best proof of scientific realism about entities.[28]

This defence of scientific realism thus avoids the problems of incommensurability, of change of meaning, that plague arguments based on inference from the best explanation.

Enough has been said to show that considerable qualifications of naive scientific realism have to be made in order for it to be coherent with much of what we know concerning the nature and history of scientific theorizing, but that, when experimentation is also taken into account, a realistic reference for postulated entities can become entirely plausible. A wide variety of scientific realisms have, in fact, been proposed in the last few years: all proponents share an emphasis on the role of reason in choice between different theories and qualify their assent with adjectives such as "conjectural,"[29] "sceptical and qualified,"[30] or "critical"[31] to distance themselves from the naive position.

(f) *Models in science.* So far, we have talked of scientific "theories" and, occasionally, of "hypotheses," as tentative, yet-to-be confirmed theories, and, even more occasionally, of "models" as part of the conceptual apparatus utilized in the sciences. Because it has come to be realized, especially since the pioneer work of Ian Ramsey,[32] that theological language (indeed the ordinary religious language of devotion and the liturgy) utilizes models over a wide range of its discourse, it is very important for understanding the relation of the ways to reality of science and religion to clarify the roles of models in each. Moreover, since models and metaphor are closely interrelated, and especially since a case can be made[33] for regarding theological language as essentially metaphorical, it is also important, as stressed by Janet Soskice in her perceptive study,[34] to be clear about the distinction between them. In general, "an object or state of affairs is a model when it is viewed in terms of its resemblance, real or hypothetical, to some other object or state of affairs";[35] or, with particular reference to science, "a model in science is a systematic analogy postulated between a phenomenon whose laws are already known and the one under investigation."[36] Note that an entity, recurrence, or state of affairs becomes a model only when characteristics read off from its source (what the model is based upon) are attributed to its subject (whatever it represents or is a model for).

Unfortunately, as Janet Soskice points out, there has often been a loose conflation of the categories of "model" and "metaphor" with a consequent loss in precision and clarity.[37] For "metaphor" is, strictly speaking, a figure of speech, in which we speak of one thing in terms suggestive of another.[38] But a model need not be linguistic at all. Naturally, model and metaphor are closely linked, for metaphors arise when we speak on the basis of models. Thus, if we are using the computer as a model for the brain, we speak metaphorically of "programming", "input" and "feedback." Of course, the linguistic presentation of a model can take the form of a metaphor as in "The brain is a computer."[39] Science makes wide and general use of models in which source and subject differ, that is, models that generate metaphorical terms that suggest an explanatory network and these are "vital at the . . . growing edges of science."[40]

Even so, are the models of science dispensable, that is, can scientific *theories* be regarded as autonomous with regard to the models used to give form to them?[41] Such a view was certainly characteristic of the positivist and hypothetico-deductive phase of the interpretation of the structure of scientific theories, when the ideal scientific (or, more precisely, physical) theory was conceived as a mathematical system with a deductive structure. But, as we saw, this idea has been superseded because of its inadequacy with reference to actual scientific practice and to the nature of its theories. Analogies cannot be dispensed with in science; they are, according to N. R. Campbell, utterly essential to theory.[42] Building a scientific theory turns out to be a matter of constructing a proper analogy, and this analogy is provided by a model, which is then the source of metaphorical theoretical terms (e.g., the corpuscular model of gases generates terms describing the mechanical interactions of billiard balls: velocity, impact, reflection, etc.). A model cannot easily be separated from its theory, and a good model is one that can be interpreted so as to allow for development of a theory to suggest new possibilities for investigation and to predict and accommodate new observations. Thus in science "the model or analogue forms the living part of the theory, the cutting edge of its projective capacity and hence, for explanatory and predictive purposes, is indispensable."[43] For not only does a good model allow logical inferences to be made about possible phenomena not already part of its original *explanandum*, but it functions rather like a metaphor does, by throwing light "forward," as it were, into new areas of investigation and by raising previously unformulable questions about those new domains.[44]

There are certain distinctive features of models in science:[45] (i) analogy or similarity between source and subject; (ii) this similarity must be of a structural kind pertaining to the basic workings or laws of the two areas; (iii) the analogy must be systematic, i.e., suggestive of connections not always immediately apparent. Models are used both to explain laws and structures in a current field and to discover new laws and structures. The use of complementary models in science, notably in atomic physics, is a forceful reminder that models, however useful, are never literal; thus each has a certain inadequacy, a situation that refutes any *naive* realism. It also indicates (and this will be important for theology) that multiple models are often not just merely permissible but often necessary in science.

The different positions taken up with respect to the relation of scientific constructs to the world (and so to scientific realism) correspond to different judgments concerning models, varying from a "low" view of them simply as helpful but of passing importance, with no commitment concerning their relation to reality (a positivist and instrumentalist "as if" view); to a realist, "high" view which sees models as an essential and permanent feature of science with a commitment to their partial but genuine ontological status ("the way things are," to varying degrees).

Both positions can include a recognition of the importance of the imagination in scientific work and of the critical role of models, and both are also aware of their limitations, but they differ in their assessment of their ontological status. The "high view" supporters[46] see scientific models as candidates for reality, as constructive and often imaginative forays into the world, that is, as reflecting reality. They accept the tension that exists between, on the one hand, the model and the metaphors it generates and, on the other, the reality it attempts to depict—a tension they regard as fruitful and conducive to openness to change in the model, and so to the growth and development of a more comprehensive theoretical framework. On this view, models are concerned with discovery, opening up the unintelligible to intelligibility, that is, with understanding the real world. They are concerned with networks of relationships, structures, and processes that are going on in the world, and invite existential commitment but only in a qualified manner — they are appropriate but can be partial and inadequate, though some models acquire over a long period a widely accepted realistic status.

But how can metaphorical theoretical terms, or any non-observational terms in a theory, be regarded as depicting reality in view of the use of models to discuss what we cannot possibly fully comprehend? Are such metaphorical terms always going to lack specifiable referents and so be irresolvably vague? This problem links up with the discussion of social theories of reference[47] that provide a buttress to the realist position, since such theories indicate how reference may be fixed without being restricted by the straitjacket of a definition and have the virtue of separating reference from *un*revisable description and grounding it instead in the experience of a continuous linguistic community. It is in this mode that Janet Soskice[48] argues for a combination of critical realism and an account of reference (in her case a social one) and concludes that "metaphors are allowable, their vagueness valuable, and their relational structure useful to theoretical accounts."[49] Metaphors are necessary for theoretical explanation in science, because by means of them "one can refer to little understood features of the natural world without laying claim to an unrevisable description of them, and this, in its theoretical stages, scientific explanation hopes to do." Moreover, metaphors generate new phases of scientific enquiry precisely because it is not words which refer but speakers using words who refer. The involvement of scientists in a continuous linguistic and experimenting community is thus essential, not only to the continuous use of theoretical terms from the time of the original introducing event[50] and so to their ability to depict reality; but also to the requirement that the models, as well as the metaphors the models generate, should be sufficiently flexible to allow the scientific enterprise to be capable of generating new enquiries. It is such a cautious "critical," "skeptical and qualified" realism concerning scientific models and metaphors, combined with this experimentational and social understanding of reference, that I am going to be concerned to relate to theological reflection on religious experience.

II. THE WORLD — IN THE LIGHT OF THE SCIENCES

If we adopt such a skeptical and qualified realist interpretation of scientific theories and models, then it behooves us to take seriously the picture of the natural, including human, world that contemporary science depicts. For that picture is the best we have for the time being and as close as we are likely to get to the reality of the natural world in the "three score years and ten" that most of us are likely to have! So let us look for a moment at the world unveiled by the sciences.

With an increasing richness and articulation of its various levels, the expansion of our knowledge of the natural world has more and more shown it to consist of a hierarchy of systems, particularly the various levels of organization in the living world: the sequence of complexity (atom . . . molecule . . . ecosystem) represents a series of levels of organization of matter in which each successive member of the series is a whole constituted of parts preceding it in the series. This raises the issue of "whether the theories and experimental laws formulated in one field of science can be shown to be special cases of theories and laws formulated in some other branch of science. If such is the case, the former branch of science is said to have been reduced to the latter."[51]

It is necessary, first, to distinguish between the hierarchy of natural *systems* and the hierarchy of the *theories of the sciences* appropriate to those systems; second, to distinguish the uncontroversial *methodological* reduction (the breaking up of a complex natural entity into its component units) that is necessary for research and comprehension, from an *epistemological* reduction (often generating, if not very clear-headedly, an *ontological* reduction) whereby scientific theories appropriate to a higher level of complexity in the hierarchy of natural systems are, it is claimed, logically translatable, in principle at least, into theories appropriate to the next level down—e.g., explaining *all* biology in terms of physics and chemistry (à la Francis Crick); or all social patterns in terms of a genetic cost-benefit calculus (à la sociobiology); or psychological events in terms of neurophysiology. In many cases, it can be shown[52] that there is an irreducible difference in conceptual structure that simply will not allow such simplistic translations and that the theories (and associated models) appropriate to the higher level have an autonomy proper to themselves. On this view, subatomic physics is *not* the paradigmatic science in terms of which the whole of the natural world, physical and biological, will one day be "explained." This does not mean that the science of one level does not depend on the best knowledge that is available from the science of the level below in the hierarchy of complexity. But it does mean that the science at each level may well develop concepts of its own appropriate and relevant to the specific behaviors, relationships, and properties that can only be seen at that level.[53]

This has interesting consequences. The first arises from noting that the hierarchy of complexity observed in the natural world today has, by means of the sciences themselves, been shown to be an evolved hierarchy in which, over long eons of terrestrial, and even astronomical, time the more complex has evolved from the less so. Thus the natural world has, through time, manifested an emergence of new kinds of organization that manifest qualities, and whose descriptions require predicates, specific for each different level. Most notable among these is the emergence of consciousness and of the self-conscious personhood of humanity.

The second consequence of the nonreductionist character of the relationships between the sciences is that we have no basis for any favored discrimination in our attribution of "reality" to the different levels in the hierarchy of complexity. There is no sense in which subatomic particles are to be graded as "more real" than, say, a bacterial cell or a human person or, even, social facts (or God?). Each level has to be regarded as real, as a cut through the totality of reality, if you like, in the sense that we have to take account of its mode of operation at that level (and woe betide us if, while analyzing the oncoming car into its component quarks and baryons, we fail to recognize the reality of the whole!). Even though our present world has evolved out of the "hot big bang" that was constituted, it seems, of entities even more elementary than those I have just referred to, yet it is still the case that we know something more and new about matter when we see its potentialities actualized in the higher levels of complexity that have evolved on the Earth, at least.

Thus it is that we now broach the concern of the second part of this lecture. Man is a natural part of the universe, and one of his characteristic activities is the exercise of religion. Now theology is the intellectual analysis of that specific human activity. When man is exercising himself in his religious and worshipping activities, he is in fact operating at a level in the hierarchy of complexity that is more intricate than any of the levels studied by the individual natural, social, and other human sciences. There are many and diverse modes of interaction involved in the religious activities of a human being: solitariness; relations with other people; reflection upon the natural world; communing with God; and subtle integrations of all of these. (Note, en passant, how the sacramental activities of the Christian church explicitly manifest and unite these multiple aspects of human life.) In human religious activities, whole persons interact with each other, with the natural world, and with the transcendent, yet immanent, Creator as the source of all that is — the One who, for the theist, gives them and the world meaning and ultimate significance. No higher level of integrated relationships in the hierarchy of natural systems can be envisaged, and theology is about the conceptual schemes (theories) and models and associated metaphors that articulate the content of this activity of the individual and of a historical community. So it should not be surprising if its theories, models, and metaphors turn out to be uniquely specific to, and characteristic of, this emergent level.

Thus we can have a legitimate placement for the activity and language of the theological enterprise as it reflects on this specifically and uniquely human activity that, involving nature, man, and God in its total integrating purview, stands at the summit of conceivable complexity and wholeness. Perhaps theology, if no longer the medieval "queen of the sciences," may at least be accorded the honors of a constitutional monarch? Be that as it may — it is the way of religion to the reality that is God to which we must now turn.

III. THE THEOLOGICAL ENTERPRISE

(a) *The current status of theology.* By the theological enterprise, I refer to the reflective and intellectual analysis of the religious experience of mankind and, in particular, of the Christian experience. The *fact* of such experience can hardly be gainsaid, especially in the twentieth century, in the light of the many studies from those of William James and C. G. Jung to the work over the last fifteen years of the Religious Experience Research Unit (Sir Alister Hardy) at Oxford, which demonstrates how unexpectedly widespread are illuminating experiences permeated by the sense of the presence of a transcendent Other, experiences that have to be categorized as religious. Moreover, all religious believers regard themselves as making meaningful assertions about a reality that man can and does encounter, a reality whose name is God in the Judeo-Christian tradition. So religion, or better "religious experience,"[54] has been and still is regarded as a path to reality.

Before we assess this claim, let us look at the state of religion in our Western world, and the state of Christian theology in particular. I shall not concern myself here with the turbulent resuscitations of fundamentalist Islam, or (less turbulent but no less influential) of moral-majority fundamentalist American evangelical Christianity, or of pre-Vatican II, almost ultramontane, Roman Catholicism that we have witnessed in the past decade. In an uncertain, risky world, when social boundaries are being obliterated, social psychologists can readily provide sociological causes for such phenomena. I am here more concerned with shifts in our knowledge, in our patterns of thought, and with the inherent dynamics of the internal development of Christian theology in recent decades—just as I earlier looked at the change in the status of science and in the philosophy of science.

The more general aspects of these changes are well known, but I must mention two before proceeding with my main task. First, there is an increasing awareness not only among Christian theologians, but also, even more, among ordinary believers that, if God is in fact the all-encompassing Reality that Christian faith proclaims, then that Reality is to be experienced in and through our actual lives as biological organisms who are persons, part of nature and society. So knowledge of nature and society can never be irrelevant to our experience of God, if he is the one whom the faith affirms, and other-worldliness is regarded as a retreat from reality or, at least, has become unfashionable (though how "other-worldiness" is to be defined is often left dangerously obscure).

Secondly, the Barthian resort of Protestants to the pure Word of God available through the scriptures and the pre-Vatican II resort by Roman Catholics to a resting entirely upon the authority of the tradition have come to be seen as routes that are not viable. For the further such ploys take us from the presumed fallibilities of our natural minds to the supposed divine authority of scripture or tradition, the closer they bring us to the question: How can we *know* that these Scriptures, this tradition, is transmitting to us the genuine word of God? Hence, there has been a new openness of both Protestant and Roman Catholic (and Anglican) theology not only to the broader streams of intellectual inquiry in our culture (including the sciences), but also to each other and to other religions. Such openness renders Christian theology liable to succumb to passing intellectual fashions and vulnerable to the kind of sociological-anthropological critiques that have also attempted to relocate, indeed to demote, the sciences in the hierarchy of knowledge. This pressure has been experienced longer by the Christian religion than by the sciences and has often had to be resisted, often not unsuccessfully. We will not linger on this parallel between the social critiques of science and religion but will concern ourselves with the sharper questions about the status of purported religious experience—namely, questions such as: Can religious experience, which is so intimate and personal and deep within the individual psyche, ever find a communicable language that could be socially effective? Or, Is talk about God valid? Or, Do theological terms refer to realities: are they about reality? Or, better, in the words of a not unfriendly critic of Christian theology, R. W. Hepburn: "The question which should be of greatest concern to the theologian is . . . whether or not the circle of myth, metaphor and symbol is a closed one: and if closed then in what way propositions about God manage to refer."[55] So formulated, the question is strikingly similar to questions that have been posed about the status of theoretical terms in science, and it plunges us immediately into an assessment of the role of models and metaphor in theology.

(b) *Models in theology.* We have already seen that the status of models in science covered the entire spectrum from naive realism via positivism and instrumentalism to a critical realism.[56] The status of theories (doctrines) and models in theology can be similarly classified:[57] "naive realism," as theological fundamentalism about received doctrines; "positivism," as biblical literalism (reliance on biblical texts as empirical data and disregard for interpretative categories); "instrumentalism," whereby religious myths and stories are either simple aids to the pursuit of policies of life by capturing the imagination and strengthening the mind,[58] or are able to evoke mystical experiences; and "critical realism," whereby theological concepts and models are partial and inadequate, but necessary and, indeed, the only ways of referring to the *reality* that is God and God's relation to humanity.

The discussion of the role of models and metaphors in theology is given an added impetus by the recognition both that they play a much wider role in religious language than had previously been commonly accepted and that they are necessary also to scientific theory construction. The recognition that religious and theological language is rich in models stems from the work of Ian Ramsey,[59] which has been much discussed and subsequently developed by others.[60] Thus, God is variously described as Father, Creator, Maker,

King, Sovereign, Shepherd, Judge; Jesus as the Christ, Messiah, Second Adam, Son of God, Redeemer, Savior; and the third *persona* of the Trinity as Holy Spirit, Holy Ghost, Comforter. The doctrine of the Trinity is thus as much metaphorical as conceptual (God as Creator, Incarnate and Immanent). The relationship of God to the world is variously depicted by means of monarchical models (God as King, Sovereign, Maker) and organic models[61] (the created order as like a garment worn by God; as the work of a potter; as an emanation of God's life-giving energy; as a manifestation of God's Wisdom or Word). The relation of God and humankind has been described in terms of models of father-son, lord-servant, mother-child, hen-chickens, lover-beloved, husband-wife, master-slave, etc. The work of Jesus Christ has, in atonement theories, been represented in models of various kinds: sacrifice, redemption, ransom, substitution, and moral example. These models are so deeply embedded in Christian language that it is extremely difficult to frame theories and concepts entirely devoid of metaphor, for even abstract words like "transcendent," "immanent," and "pan-en-theism" partake of spatial metaphors. But as this widespread use of metaphor is now seen to be also the case in science more than had previously been recognized, the theological enterprise is not thereby prematurely ruled out of court.

The *similarities* between theological and scientific models noted variously by a number of authors may be summarized as follows:

(i) Both kinds of models are generally speaking analogical and, more particularly, metaphorical and not explicitly descriptive (which would only be possible if we knew reality as it is in itself). They are extensible therefore to new situations and have to be comprehended as units. A critical, or skeptical and qualified, realism is appropriate in both domains.

(ii) In both science and theology, the models are "candidates for reality" that are reformable and are as close as we can get to speaking accurately of reality: they are not literal pictures, but they are more than useful fictions. They are both representations, for particular purposes, of aspects of reality that are not directly accessible to us. They reflect reality and are to be taken seriously but not literally. They are partial and inadequate — and as good as we can have for the time being. So formulation of models in both science and theology partakes of the nature of discovery and of increasing intelligibility. In science it is the entities and structures of the natural world that are discovered and rendered intelligible. In religious experience, and in its theological articulation, it is the basic phenomena of lived existence, and the human response to the search for meaning and intelligibility in the context of both God and nature and other men, the relation of nature-man-and-God, that is discovered and rendered intelligible.

(iii) Models in both science and theology are concerned less with picturing objects than with depicting processes, relations, and structures (i.e., patterns of relationship). What matter is "in itself," and what God is "in himself" are left as unknown and unknowable. Known modes of relation are used to model the unknown in both science and religion.

(iv) Both kinds of model, scientific and religious, are formulated and propounded in the context of a community that is a living tradition of reference back to originating experiments and experiences, and one that has developed and is still developing language and symbols to maintain this continuity of intelligibility.[62] The continuous linguistic community is vital to social reference in science, to the introducing events that named its entities and terms. Similarly, in the Christian community, key words and concepts go back to events and disclosures in the biblical sources or to church councils that resolved and formulated the outcome of often intensive debate and controversies about valid interpretation and theological language — and so about the appropriateness of various models (e.g., about the way the divine and human were both present in Jesus the Christ and the relation of the *personae* of the Trinity). Furthermore, experiences of God continue to occur, and the interpretation of both these and past such experiences are communicated to, and many endure to be meaningful in, that continuing community.

The *differences* between the use of models in science and theology have also been discerned by various authors and include the following:

(i) Models and their associated metaphors are crucial and critical for theology, and "the broadest type of theological model [the metaphysical model of the relations of nature-man-and-God] . . . is without limit and hence unfalsifiable. This is the root-metaphor or original model."[63] Here the reference is to the model of God as personal, transcendent Creator, immanent in and transforming his creation and especially man — i.e., of God as Creator, Redeemer, Sanctifier. This biblical root-metaphor of God as the personal source of all being, "in whom we live and move and have our being," has a comprehensive role at the summit of a hierarchy of theological models and metaphors explicating religious experience. No scientific theory fills this role in science. Hence religious models and their associated metaphors are more influential than and less subservient to abstract theories (doctrines) than are models in relation to theories in science.

(ii) Religious models have a strong affective function evoking moral and spiritual response, so much so that some writers, impressed by this undoubted feature, have been led to underplay the cognitive role of theological models. Thus, T. Fawcett depicts models in science as "observer" models that explain, represent, and predict and contrasts these with the "participator" models of religion that "enable us to think of the cosmos in such a way that man as a personal being is able to see himself as a fitting part of the whole. . . . The personal model ensures that the cosmos is perceived as personal."[64] Indisputably, theological models do have a component of evaluation and an evocative ability that is lacking in scientific models. Theological models affect our feelings and provoke us to action: they evoke commitment and self-involvement.

Some authors infer from this that the reality depicted by theological models is simply that of the human condition with its need for faith and trust. But, as Janet Soskice asks "Faith in what? Trust in what?"[65] For the models stir the will and emotions because of their cognitive content, their reference to that which makes demands on our will and evokes our emotion. However affective and personal they may be in their effect, theological models purport to be explanatory. As she rightly asserts:

> Typically Christians respond to the models of their religious tradition not because they take them to be elegant and compelling means of describing the human condition but because they believe them in some way to depict states and relations of a transcendent kind.[66]

In other words, Christian believers take their models to depict reality, otherwise they would be affectively and personally ineffectual and inoperative. Yet the reality such believers seek to depict is one that the creature cannot claim to describe as it is in itself — *ex hypothesi* God as transcendent is beyond all explicit depiction whether by language or visual image. How can such an intuition be reconciled with the philosophical pressure to show how theological propositions actually *refer*, that theological models are depicting reality?

(c) *Reference: the mediated and direct experience of God.* We recall that what established reality of reference for terms and entities in scientific theories and models were: (i) the social chain in a continuous linguistic community that could anchor our present usage of a term in the original introducing event, in which (say) a physical magnitude (e.g., electricity) or entity (e.g., an electron) was referred to by saying that it was "whatever caused this state of affairs"; and (ii) the repeatable experiments in which such entities could be continued to be so referred to, together with new experimentation in which such entities are used as tools, so enabling them to operate as causes and their causal powers to be understood. Can such a linkage, by a linguistic social chain and in (at least, putatively) contemporary experience, be established for references to God in theological models and metaphors?

Before tackling this question let us remind ourselves of what metaphorical referring language can and cannot do. For,

> to be a realist about the referent is to be a fallibilist about knowledge of the referent. . . . So the theist may be mistaken in his beliefs *about* the source and cause of all . . . for fixing a referent does not on this account guarantee that the referent meets a particular description.[67]

The distinction between referring to God and describing him is vital to this whole theological critical realist position. It is here that negative theology and positive theology meet: the former recognizes that, having referred to God, whatever we say will be fallible and revisable and *ex hypothesi* inadequate; the latter that to say nothing is more misleading than to say something, and that then we have to speak metaphorically. So we have good grounds for affirming that metaphorical language, the language expound-

ing the theological models that explicate religious experience, can be referential and can depict reality without at the
same time being naively and unrevisably descriptive. And
this character theological models share with scientific models
of the natural world. So if we say, for example, that God
is Father, we would speak of an actual real relationship of
God to man that could be indicated in no other way. According to this view, we may fairly hope to speak realisti-
cally of God through revisable metaphor and model.

Now the quest can begin! As has been well said: "Christian life is an adventure, a voyage of discovery, a journey,
sustained by faith and hope, towards a final and complete
communion with the Love at the heart of all things."[68]

However this adventure, this journey, although inevitably alone, for the individual, has been explored ahead of
us. For there certainly have been, and still are, individuals
and communities who affirm they have experienced God.
There are also continuous religious communities with a
long history that can command immense resources which
they make available to the individual in his or her quest for
God. What significance may be given to those experiences
and those resources in the light of our analysis of reference,
model, and metaphor in theological language? We recall
that in the contemporary scientific community, according
to the thesis already elaborated, referring successfully to an
entity, say an electron, can be achieved by affirming that
one is referring to that which causes (say) this galvanometer
needle to be deflected or this cloud chamber track to take
such and such a path. And this can be achieved without
knowing what electrons are "in themselves." Given the
parallels between the use of models and metaphors in scientific and theological language, it seems to me to be equally
legitimate to affirm that God can be "that which causes this
particular experience now (or in the past) in me (or in
others)." The more recurrent and widespread the experi-

ences in question, the more secure the reference, and so the reality, of that which is referred to.[69] However, the dissemination of such recognition of the validity of the God-reference in individuals' experience can only be slow, with much sifting and attestation, because any one individual's claim can always be contested (and other—psychological, psychiatric, sociological, etc.—causes assigned).

Hence the kind of critical theological realism we have been developing places at the center past and present religious experience, the continuous community, and an interpretative tradition. Reference is grounded in the seminal, initiating experiences of individuals and communities when references to God were first made in the "introducing events"—and the community then, and continuously since, provides the links of referential usage and repeated and new experiences that enable us today to refer to what the initiators referred to, even though we may have revised our models through continuous reinterpretation ("development of doctrine"). In that process of initiation and reinterpretation, some individuals and communities will command assent, acquire authority, more than others—by virtue of their presence at the initial, introducing, referring event(s) or experience, by virtue of their intellectual preeminence in the interpretative process of more widespread and universal experiences through the ages, and by virtue of the men and women they were and are. Through such transmitted experience, all can participate in the special, definitive experiences of God of the few and, once these have been made communally accessible, they become available as a resource for all. This general assent continues in strength only if current experiences of at least *some* members of the community continue to be congruent with the earlier ones. So there are guides to bring harmony to the cacophony of voices that claim to speak of that reality which is God. None will be infallible, but a number will certainly be surer; and some will have linguistic and communal contexts that speak to our condition more than others — their models and metaphors will be taken into the common currency of usage by the generality of Christians.

Now metaphor, and its integrated form as model, is always implying "this is like that" *and at the same time* "this is *not* like the (same) that" — there is always an "is and is not" quality about metaphor.[70] So that we might hope for a coherent and fruitful complementarity between, on the one hand, the mediated and, on the other hand, the direct experience of God of humankind, in general — and, in the Christian community, between, on the one hand, positive theology ("revelation and reason") and on the other hand, the content of contemplative and mystical experiences.

In positive theology, the *via affirmativa*, we may be "cribb'd, cabined, and confined" by the linguistic and cultural context in which we make our enquiry, but it is God whom the faithful really refer to and discover in the Christian experience, just as it is nature we really refer to and discover in the sciences. The Christian experience also includes the more diffuse experiences of God through reflection on the "way things are," for God is Creator and is still creating, his nature and being are still discernible through his ways with the world. It is the world — and in this I include nature, society, personal relations, and the products of human creativity in the visual arts and literature and music — that informs our models and metaphors that refer to God; these latter are indeed the best "theories" that we can have though they can never adequately describe him. Here perhaps the wider experiences (e.g., of order, of causality, of rationality in the cosmos, and of contingency) that figure so much in the classical "proofs" of God's existence come into their own as the universal experiences that, when reflected upon, lead human beings to refer to "God." "This men call God," in Aquinas' phrase. These are two modes by which God is experienced and referred to in "positive" theology: the tradition of the community, with social links back to the introducing events, and through reflection on the "world" (i.e., the interplay of revelation with reason in the more classical terminology). These two continuously interact and enrich each other and constitute together the thrust of positive theology that is explicated in metaphor.

Metaphor, as we have seen, inevitably and implicitly recognizes in its very use its own inherent limitations — that what the reality of God, in this instance, is in itself is beyond the power of language to express. It is at this juncture that there has to be invoked the resources of the contemplative and mystical experience in which silence and darkness descend, and the felt presence of God renders the wisest dumb — that movement into those depths of the unconscious, where God dwells in silence. Such experiences are the necessary corrective, both in each individual and in the community, to saying too much, the temptation to justify the jibe of E. M. Forster about "poor, talkative Christianity." Christian theology too readily forgets that there is an "is not" in all metaphor, not least in those that relate to God. For that God to which, in the exposition I have been attempting, our theological models and metaphors really refer is a Reality beyond all explicit knowing. But if the models of God as Father and the supreme model of God in the person of Jesus the Christ have any validity at all, we can know that this reality that is God acts to meet us in the silence and the darkness.

In describing their experiences, Christian contemplatives and mystics have used images, models, and metaphors that have their roots in the Judeo-Christian heritage (for example, *inter alia*: "dark night of the soul"; "cloud of unknowing"; "spiritual marriage"). So that, private though these experiences were, they are not unavailable to other Christians who have to weigh and test their worth as general coinage — and some, over the centuries, become authoritative in the sense that others trust them. Thereby the experiences of the contemplative or mystic become truly "catholic" in the Vicentian sense of what has been believed everywhere, always, and by all (*quod ubique, quod semper, quod ab omnibus creditum est*), passing the test of ecumenicity, antiquity, and consent — and thereby enriching the lives of others in the community who have not participated in the seminal, originating experiences, whether past or contemporary. The language used can properly be said to refer to God, to depict his reality, but not in any unrevisable way. Thus, in one sense, the Christian mystic is your true critical realist — compelled to be aware both of the reality of God and of the utter inadequacy of human speech about him. Perhaps we should call such a one a contemplative, critical realist, one entirely convinced that the source of his or her experiences is the God who is the source and cause of all that is.

So the nature of our talk about God makes it essential for both the individual believer and for the community of believers to recognize that the way to the reality that is God should be followed in *both* its modes: the mediated, positive way, the *via affirmativa*, through the world and the revelation transmitted through the community; and the direct way of contemplation and silence. Both are for each and all of us, though no doubt in varying proportions and degrees of intensity.

IV. CONCLUSION

I hope I have been able to demonstrate that any judgment of science and religion as two far apart, flanking, and limiting routes of human exploration into reality is at the best superficial and at worst disastrously misleading. No more can we see science as, on the one hand, all objective, rationalistic, and realistic and religion, on the other, as subjective, emotional, and possibly hallucinatory. For the scientific and theological enterprises share alike the tools of groping humanity — our stock of words, ideas, and images that have been handed down, tools that we refashion in our own way for our own times in the light of experiment and experience to relate to the natural world and that are available, with God's guidance, to steer our own paths from birth to death.

There is a hierarchy of order in the natural world, and, if God is the reality that Christians believe he is, the ways of science and of Christian faith must always, in my view, be ultimately converging. I cannot but see, in the light of this, the scientific and theological enterprises as interacting and mutually illuminating approaches to reality. Since the theological enterprise refers to a higher level in the hierarchy of complexity, the interaction of nature, man, and God, it will have to take continuous account of models developed to expound the new knowledge of the sciences of the less complex levels below. It will have to listen to and adapt to, but not be subservient to, such new discoveries concerning the realities of the natural world (as I shall try to illustrate in my second lecture). Similarly the sciences, which are *human* creative activities and have repercussions that are sometimes destructive of nature and society, will have to be more willing than in the past to see their models of reality as partial and applicable at restricted levels only in the multiform intricacies of the real and always to be related to the wider intimations of reality that are vouchsafed to mankind. It was to these intimations that two significant writers have turned in passages full of meaning for our times; one has followed that hard way of Christian faith through suffering and desolation, the other the path of science through the thicket of the natural. Both ways are needed.

First, then, the Christian, Aleksandr Solzhenitsyn's conclusion to that 1983 Templeton Prize address. It is only from the high vantage point, *sub specie aeternitatis*, of the vision of God that the ways to the real world, including our real selves, can be discerned and, with the grace of God himself, be followed. Thus Solzhenitsyn:

> Our life consists not in the pursuit of material success but in the quest of worthy spiritual growth. Our entire earthly existence is but a transitional stage in the movement toward something higher, and we must not stumble and fall, nor must we linger fruitlessly on one rung of the ladder. Material laws alone do not explain our life or give it direction. The laws of physics and physiology will never reveal the indisputable manner in which the Creator constantly, day in and day out, participates in the life of each of us, unfailingly granting us the energy of existence; when this assistance leaves us, we die. In the life of our entire planet, the Divine Spirit moves with no less force: this we must grasp in our dark and terrible hour.

And, finally, a voice "from below," from one following the path of the really natural to the naturally Real that gave it being — the words of Loren Eiseley, the American biologist:

> It is not sufficient any longer to listen at the end of a wire to the rustlings of galaxies; it is not enough even to examine the great coil of DNA in which is coded the very alphabet of life. These are our extended perceptions. But beyond lies the great darkness of the ultimate Dreamer, who dreamed the light and the galaxies. Before act was, or substance existed, imagination grew in the dark. Man partakes of that ultimate wonder and creativeness. As we turn from the galaxies to the swarming cells of our own being, which toil

for something, some entity beyond their grasp, let us remember man, the self-fabricator who came across an ice age to look into the mirrors and the magic of science. Surely he did not come to see himself or his wild visage only. He came because he is at heart a listener and a searcher for some transcendent realm beyond himself. This he has worshiped by many names, even in the dismal caves of his beginning. Man, the self-fabricator, is so by reason of gifts he had no part in devising.[71]

2

God's Action in the Real World[1]

Towards the end of the first lecture, I urged that the scientific and theological enterprises were interacting and mutually illuminating approaches to reality. I also suggested that the theological enterprise refers to the highest level in the hierarchy of the complexities that constitute reality, namely the relation nature-man-and-God, and so some, at least, of the concepts, models, and metaphors appropriate to it may well not be reducible to those applicable to lower levels in the hierarchy of natural systems. There are in religious experience, and in the experience of the Christian community with which I am most concerned, concepts, models, and metaphors which have a life of their own, a history of their own, and an impact of their own within their own thought world. The terms of religious discourse are often very subtle and intricate in their relations with the many levels in the life of mankind, but, because they refer to a total activity of human beings in community in their total relationships with the natural world, they must not be prematurely reduced away to some lower-level scientific description. What we must do is set these "religious" affirmations, their ways of depicting the world, their understandings of the world and of man in the world, *alongside* the changing perspective of man in the world that the sciences engender through studying the individual levels which the natural hierarchy of systems displays. Theology should be neither immune from the changing outlook of the sciences of man and nature nor should it be captive to them. Theology, I said, will have to listen to and adapt to, but not be subservient to, new understandings of the natural world afforded by the sciences. For both religion and science seek intelligibility within a framework of meaning and, if my approach in the first lecture has proven acceptable, both are concerned with an understanding of reality inevitably articulated by means of model and metaphor.

Today, after more than three hundred years of the scientific revolution in man's understanding of the natural world, including himself, it seems to me proper to enquire what effects this unparalleled expansion of knowledge and extension of consciousness should have on our way of modelling the relation of God, the ineffable, to the world as *so* known. Thus, any affirmations about God's relation to the world, any doctrine of creation, if it is not to become vacuous and sterile, must be about the relation of God to, the creation by God of, the world which the natural sciences describe. It seems to me that this is not a situation where Christian, or indeed *any*, theology has any choice — and, indeed, ought to expect to have any. For the scientific perspective on the world affords the most reliable available answers to questions men have always asked about it: What is there? What goes on? How does it change? Why does it change?

Any theological account of God's relation to the world is operating in an intellectual vacuum, not to say cultural ghetto, if it fails to relate its affirmations to the answers to these questions that the natural sciences have been able to develop. It is true that theology, the intellectual ordering of the religious experience, is concerned with wider and deeper questions of overall intelligibility and personal and social meaning than the natural sciences as such. But *these* fundamental questions cannot be asked at all without directing them to the world as we best know and understand it, that is, as seen in the light of the sciences.

We shall now, therefore, consider certain features of the contemporary scientific perspective and then ask whether that perspective should influence, or at least allow us to choose between, models of the ways in which we may conceive of God's relation to and action in the real world.

I. THE TRANSFORMATION OF THE SCIENTIFIC WORLDVIEW THROUGH TWENTIETH-CENTURY PHYSICS AND COSMOLOGY

By the end of the nineteenth century the absolutes of space, time, object, and determinism were apparently securely enthroned in an unmysterious, mechanically-determined world, basically simple in structure at the atomic level and, statistically at least, unchanging in form. Yet, within a few decades at the beginning of the twentieth century, there was a "veritable Götterdammerung" of these gods of absolute space, time, object, and determinism.[2] What is the new worldview, then, that dawns to succeed this Götterdammerung?

Perhaps the most distinctive feature of the modern scientific worldview is the converging perspective of a number of quite different sciences on the world as being in *process of evolution*. The cosmologists and astrophysicists have shown us how, from a time of the order of ten billion (10^{10}) years ago, a primeval, unimaginably condensed, mass of fundamental particles could have been transformed, at the same time expanding, into the present observable universe — with its 10^9 galaxies each containing 10^8-10^{11} stars (plus associated planets) — of a size such that light is reaching our planet that set out on its path before the Sun and the Earth were formed. We shall later take note of how there have emerged those complex organizations of matter that are living, including ourselves. "Cosmic evolution has been attended by a great increase in *the richness and diversity of forms.* . . . This is an inventive process and is one that is still continuing."[3] As matter has coalesced into more and more complex forms, new and very different kinds of behavior and properties have emerged. Time has been given new meaning as the "carrier or locus of innovative change",[4] a role scarcely envisaged as a possibility within that Newtonian absolute time which flowed "equably without relation to anything external."[5]

A notable aspect of this picture is the seamless character of the web which has been spun on the loom of time; the process is continuous from beginning to end and at no point does the modern natural scientist have to invoke any nonnatural causes to explain what he observes or infers about the past. His explanations are usually in terms of concepts, theories, and mechanisms which he can confirm by, or infer from, present-day experiments. The scientist's confidence is sufficiently well based that it would be extremely unwise for any proponent of theism to attempt to find any gaps to be closed by the intervention of some nonnatural agent, such as a god.

Looking back, we now see that the beginning of the twentieth century initiated a series of fundamental changes in the scientific perspective on the world. *Then*—that is, in the half-century terminating at 1900—nature was regarded as simple in structure: *now*, we know it is enormously complex, consisting of a hierarchy of levels of organization.

Then, as we saw earlier, the natural world was regarded as mechanically determined and predictable from any given state by means of laws of all-embracing scope: *now*, the world is regarded rather as the scene of the interplay of chance and of statistical, as well as causal, uniformity in which there is indeterminacy at the *micro*-level and unpredictability at the *macro*-level, especially that of the biological.

Then, in spite of Darwinism, the natural world was still largely regarded as static in form: *now*, it is discovered to be dynamic — always in process — a nexus of evolving forms, essentially incomplete, inexhaustible in its potential for change, and open to the future.

Then, the world seemed to be decomposable into simple subunits: *now*, a sense of mystery at the quality of the known and the quantity of the unknown has been engendered by the depths of reality encountered at the edges of experimental and theoretical enquiry.

It becomes clear that we have in our times witnessed an unparalleled leap in the expansion of human consciousness of the world. If the world were a closed system, we would expect an ultimate convergence in our knowledge as it accumulates, but nothing like this seems to be happening. Our awareness of our ignorance grows in parallel with, indeed faster than, the growth in our knowledge. Yet one is struck, as John Polkinghorne, until recently Professor of Mathematical Physics at Cambridge and now an Anglican priest, puts it,

> by the fact . . . that mathematics, which essentially is the abstract free creation of the human mind, repeatedly provides the indispensable clue to the understanding of the physical world. This happening is so common a process that most of the time we take it for granted. At root it creates the *possibility* of science, of our understanding the workings of the world.[6]

Our unity with the rest of the biological world should hardly need emphasizing in these days of ecological concern. But awareness of our dependence on and involvement in the cosmic processes is relatively recent. The values of the fundamental constants (velocity of light, electronic charge, etc.) determine the kind of physical world in which we live, and it turns out that, if (for example) the proton-proton interaction were only slightly different, then all of the protons in the universe would have turned into inert helium in the early stages of expansion of the galaxies. As Sir Bernard Lovell put it "No galaxies, no stars, no life would have emerged. It would be a universe forever unknowable by living creatures. The existence of a remarkable and intimate relationship between man, the fundamental constants of nature and the initial moments of space and time, seems to be an inescapable condition of our presence here . . .".[7]

The material units of the universe—the subatomic particles, the atoms, and the molecules they can form—are the fundamental entities constituted in their matter-energy-space-time relationships, and are such that they have built-in, as it were, the potentiality of becoming organized in that special kind of complex system we call living and, in particular, in the system of the human-brain-in-the-human-body which displays conscious activity. In man, the stuff of the universe has become cognizing and self-cognizing.

Briefly, because we have evolved to observe it, our universe is a *cognizable* one; this places restrictions on the kind of universe it could be out of the range of all possible universes (the so-called "anthropic principle").[8] This simply expresses in a new way the old assertion that the universe in which we exist is contingent. Moreover, far from man's presence in the universe being a curious and inexplicable surd, we find we are remarkably and intimately related to it on the basis of this contemporary scientific evidence, which is "indicative of a far greater degree of man's total involvement with the universe"[9] than ever before envisaged.

This brings us to another major speculation of cosmologists. It is clear that, in tracing the history of the universe back to the point ca. 10^{10} years ago when all its mass is postulated as having been concentrated into a relatively small space (of the size of a lecture room or less!), there comes a point beyond which the laws of physics, as we know them, cannot be applied. Even so, this does not exclude the possibility that there is another side to the "hot big bang," away from our own. Beyond this point, when the "universe is squeezed through a knot hole,"[10] all physical constants and entities might be different. If so, we have to envisage the possibility that our universe is but one amongst a cycle of universes and just happens to be one in which the physical constants (and even the physical laws) are such that living matter, and thus man, could, in time, appear within it, and so be cognizable.

So it is that we come to stress the particularity of our universe: there are certain basic given features — the fundamental constants, particles, and laws which limit what can eventually be realized through its evolutionary processes. Even though these limitations are not "necessary" in the sense of being features of all worlds that may have existed (or will do so), yet for us they constitute the givenness of our existence, of *its* "necessity." This givenness does not confine the open future in a universe in which dynamic processes lead to the emergence of new complex entities of distinctive qualities and activities that include not only biological life, but also the whole life of man. Moreover it is the very *givenness* of the parameters of the milieu of human life which make human freedom and human perception possible. So in this more general sense too, the cosmic order is a necessary prerequisite of conscious personal existence as we know it in human beings.

(The foregoing is not tied to the validity of the "hot big bang" account of the origin of the observable universe but only to the empirically observed evolving, emergent character whereby its processes generate new complexities.)

Because we are *critical* realists, we must take this perspective on the world afforded by physics and cosmology seriously but not too literally. This means that in thinking how it might influence our models of God's relation to and action in the world, it is only the broadest, general features, and these the most soundly established, that we must reckon with. But it will be *to* the world so described by these sciences that our theological questionings must refer, and it is *in* the world so described that we seek meaning. We must be clear from the outset that in saying that God is, and that God is Creator, we do not affirm that he/she is any ordinary "cause" in the physical nexus of the universe itself—otherwise God would be neither explanation or possible meaning. He, to drop the feminine personal pronoun (at least for the moment), cannot be the old "God of the gaps." *Ex hypothesi*, God's uniqueness and distinction from the world ensures that nothing in the world itself, such as might "fill" one of its causal gaps, can ever be a totally satisfactory and true image of his all-embracing Reality. The doctrine of creation affirms that any particular event or entity would not happen, or would not *be* at all, were it not for the sustaining creative will and activity of God. This fundamental "otherness" of God in his own inscrutable, unsurpassable, and ultimately incomprehensible Being is essential to what we mean by God. Referred to by the predicate *transcendent*, this is an inexpungable element of the Judeo-Christian (and Islamic) experience of God. Let us now look at some of the implications for our models of God-and-the-world that arise from the aspects of the scientific worldview I have just indicated.

(a) The sense of God's *transcendence* is itself reinforced by the demonstration through physics and cosmology that vast tracts of matter-energy-space-time have, and probably will, exist without any human being to observe them—and this will be further compounded if it indeed turns out to be the case that this "present" observable universe is but one of a "run" of possible universes. The excessively anthropocentric cosmic outlook of medieval, and even of Newtonian, man is thereby healthily restored to that more sober assessment which characterizes the Psalms and the Wisdom literature, and some of the prophets. For, when God finally answers Job out of the whirlwind,[11] it is not to justify his actions with respect to him, but simply to point to the whole range of the created order and to ask Job if he, as man, took any part in the nonhuman processes of creation, both past and present.

(b) *Time*, in modern relativistic physics, is an integral and basic aspect of nature: space and time have to be mutually defined in interlocking relationships and both are related to definitions of mass and energy, themselves interconvertible. So matter-energy-space-time constitute the *created* order. Hence, on any theistic view, time itself has to be regarded as owing its existence to God, as Augustine perceived in addressing God thus:

> It is therefore true to say that when you had not made anything there was no time, because time itself was of your making. And no time is co-eternal with you, because you never change: whereas, if time never changed, it would not be time. . . . Let them [those who ask the question "What was God doing before he made heaven and earth?"] see, then, that there cannot possibly be time without creation. . . . Let them understand that before all time began you are the eternal Creator of all time, and that no time and no created thing is co-eternal with you, even if any created thing is outside time.[12]

It is this "owing its existence to God" that is the essential core of the idea of Creation which concerns the relationship of all the created order, including time itself, to its Creator — its Sustainer and Preserver. Thus the fundamental "otherness" of God must include his transcendence of time.

(c) Nevertheless, there *is* an important feature which the scientific perspective inevitably reintroduces into this idea of creation. It is the realization, now made explicit, that the cosmos which is sustained and held in being by God is a cosmos which has always been in process of producing new emergent forms of matter—it is a *creatio continua*, as it has long been called in Christian theology. God creates continuously—"all the time," as we would say. The scientific perspective of a cosmos that manifests emergence of the new reemphasizes that dynamic element in our understanding of God's relation to the world which was, even if obscured, always implicit in the Hebrew conception of a "living God."

The sciences now see no breaks in the causal and temporal nexus of the evolution of the cosmos, or of life on the Earth, and thus rule out any "God of the gaps" to fill out any current scientific lacunae. Thus we must conceive of God as creating *in* the whole process from beginning to end, through and through, or he cannot be involved at all. It is not so much a question of primary and secondary causes, as classically expounded, but rather that the natural, causal, creative nexus of events *is* itself God's creative action. It is this that the attribution of *immanence* to God in his world must now be taken to convey. God is not some kind of diffuse "spiritual" gas permeating everything (like the discarded ether of the nineteenth century), but all-that-is in its actual processes *is* God manifest in his mode as continuous Creator. This also makes intelligible that striking rationality of the created order, referred to above, which makes it amenable to mathematical interpretation. For if God is at least fully personal, and so rational, his creation in its ultimate depths will be the embodiment of this aspect of his character. So a new stress is required on the *immanence* of God (the "sacrament of the present moment"?[13]) in the light of the scientific understanding of the world, and this demands to be reconciled with our profound and not-to-be-set-aside intuition of God's otherness in himself, his transcendence.

In order to bring together these two conceptions of tran-

scendence over and immanence in creation, one can resort
to a *spatial model*, the "space" of different kinds of distinction, as in a Venn diagram. Because there is no part of the
world where God is not active and present in the events and
processes themselves, and because there is infinitely more to
God's being than the world, we could say that the world
is *in God*, there is nothing in the world not in God. This
understanding of God's relation to the world is sometimes
called "pane*n*theism," which has been defined[14] as the belief
that the Being of God includes and penetrates the whole
universe, so that every part of it exists in him, but that his
Being is more than, and is not exhausted by, the universe.

   This spatial metaphor can be developed into what I think
is a more fruitful *biological model* based on human procre-
ation. The concept of God as Creator has, in the past, been
too much dominated by a stress on the externality of God's
creative acts — he is regarded as creating something external
to himself, just as the male fertilizes the ovum from outside. But mammalian females, at least, experience creation
within themselves; the growing embryo resides within the
female body. This is a proper corrective to the masculine
picture — it is an analogy of God creating the world within
herself, we would have to say. This is yet another of the
prices we pay for having in the past been more ready to
predicate of God the active, powerful, external adjectives,
conventionally and inaccurately associated with masculinity,
rather than the more passive, responsive, internal adjectives,
equally conventionally and inaccurately associated with femi-
ninity. God creates a world that is, in principle and in origin, other than "himself" but creates it, the world, within
"herself."

   (d) The demise of determinism in its strict Laplacean
form has not vitiated entirely the concept of causality. But
we now have a picture of the world as possessing a more
open-ended character, a world in which there is a much

looser coupling between any two given events and in which
science sees rather interlocking networks of statistical relationships, both at the subatomic level because of the significance in that domain of the Heisenberg Uncertainty Principle, and in the macroscopic world of biology and the
cosmos, because of the sheer complexity of structures and
the multiplicity of operative factors. A certain openness,
"looseness" even, is attributable to the structures and relational networks that constitute the natural world, and this
entails limitations on predictability. There is a degree of
openness about the future, especially in the realm of the living where separate organisms operate individualistically,
most notably *homo sapiens*. So the concept of God as the
deterministic Law-Giver prescribing *all* in advance seems inadequate and even false, and we begin to search for metaphors associated rather with probing experimentation, exploration, and improvisation, as representing more appropri-
ately what God is up to in his continuous creative activity.

(e) Finally, if we take the suggestion that this universe
(cognizable by us) is only one amongst a possible "run" of
such universes, must we say it is by chance that it, and we,
exist? We shall return to this question later in connection
with the so-called role of "chance" in biological evolution,
and its theological significance.

II. THE WORLDVIEW OF BIOLOGY

Some of the features of the world of living organisms
that modern biology has discerned accord with some of
those derived from physics and cosmology, but others are
distinctive.

(a) The *continuity* of the biological processes of evolution
follows on from that of the cosmological processes producing stars such as the Sun and its satellite planet, Earth. The

continuities of biological evolution extend now to the molecular domain, where increasingly the principles that govern the emergence of self-reproducing macromolecular systems are understood both kinetically (Eigen and colleagues at Göttingen) and thermodynamically (Prigogine and colleagues at Brussels). I will not present here the overwhelming evidence for the interconnectedness through time of all living organisms originating from one or a few primeval simple forms; I will take it for granted as the agreed view of informed, professional biologists of all creeds, in all kinds of society. (The *mechanism* of this evolutionary process is another matter, to which we shall shortly come). Again the "gaps" in the scientific account of this evolution of the multiplicity of living forms, that scientists yesterday thought they detected, continue to have the habit of being closed by the work of scientists today—and those of today will, no doubt, share the same fate tomorrow. The "gaps" into which any god may be inserted go on diminishing. For we see a world in process that is continuously capable, through its own inherent properties and natural character, of producing new living forms. In fact evolution is the process *par excellence* of the manifestation of emergence. This is the inbuilt creative potentiality of all-that-is, which we have now to see *as* God at work continuously creating in and through the stuff of the world he had endowed with those very potentialities. So again we find cause to stress God's immanence in the created order, or rather, the creating order, and consequently to affirm pan*en*theism, to maintain also his transcendence.

(b) We referred to a certain looseness in the causal coupling that physics describes. This feature of the world of science becomes more noticeable in the *open-ended character of biological evolution*. In retrospect each emergence of a new form of the organization of living matter is, in principle, intelligible to us now as the lawful consequence of a con-

catenation of random events. This involvement of randomness means that, although in retrospect the development is
intelligible (at least in principle) to modern science, yet in
prospect the development would not have been strictly predictable. The development of the world as a whole has not
unfolded a predetermined sequence of events, like the development of a mammalian embryo from the fertilized ovum.
As Dobzhansky put it: "The chief characteristic, or at any
rate one of the characteristics, of progressive evolution, is
its open-endedness. Conquest of new environments and ac-
quisition of new ways of life create opportunities for further evolutionary developments."[15] As one goes up the
scale of biological evolution the open-ended character, unpredictability, and creativity of the process becomes more
and more focused in the activity of the biological individual. For in the biological sequence, the increase of complexity, which also occurs in the non-living world of molecular
systems, in the living becomes increasingly accompanied by
an increase in consciousness, culminating in human self-
consciousness, the power of language, and rationality. This
aspect of the process reaches its apogee in man's creativity
and his sense of freedom in taking responsibility for his de-
cisions. Such a perspective on evolution therefore still at-
tributes a special significance to the emergence of human
beings in and from the material universe but recognizes that
they have arrived by means of an open-ended, trial-and-
error exploration of possibilities — an exploration devoid
neither of false trails and dead ends nor, as consciousness
emerges, immune from pain, suffering, and struggle.

If we were right tentatively to see God, as it were, exploring in creation, exploiting opportunities, then we begin
to get here a hint of an involvement by God in his creation that involves putting his purposes at risk — an involvement that, in a human context, might well be described as
suffering.

(c) *The mechanism of biological evolution* can be interpreted to reinforce this hint or intuition. That mechanism, of "natural selection" in its neo-Darwinian form, shaped by post-Darwinian genetics, is simply as François Jacob, the French, Nobel-prizewinning, molecular biologist has put it:

> First, that all organisms, past, present or future, descend from one or several rare living systems which arose spontaneously. Second, that species are derived from one another by natural selection of the best procreators.[16]

So the processes by which new species appear is a process of *new life through death of the old*. It involves a degree of competition and struggle in nature which has often offended man's moral and aesthetic sensibilities. It has taken modern biologists to restore the balance in our view of the organic world by reminding us, as Simpson puts it: "To generalise . . . that natural selection is over-all and even in a figurative sense the outcome of struggle is quite unjustified under the modern understanding of the process. . . . Struggle is sometimes involved, but it usually is not. . . . Advantage in differential reproduction is usually a peaceful process in which the concept of struggle is really irrelevant."[17]

The death of old organisms is a prerequisite for the appearance of new ones. There is indeed a kind of "structural logic" about all this, for we cannot conceive, in a lawful, nonmagical universe, of any way for new structural complexity to appear except by utilizing structures already existing, either by way of modification (as in the evolutionary process) or of incorporation (as in feeding). Thus the law of "new life through death of the old" is inevitable in a world composed of common "building blocks," but in biological evolution this does not happen without pain and suffering and both seem unavoidable. For death, pain, and

the risk of suffering are intimately connected with the possibilities of new life, in general, and of the emergence of
conscious, and especially human, life, in particular. Moreover, the very order and impersonality of the physical cosmos which makes pain and suffering inevitable for conscious and self-conscious creatures is, at the same time, also
the prerequisite of their exercise of freedom as persons.
Again, it seems hard to avoid the paradox that "natural
evil" is a necessary prerequisite for the emergence of free,
self-conscious beings. But if it is necessary, and God is involved "in, with, and under" his creation, cannot we say
again we have here a hint of *God suffering* with his creation
to bring it to its fulfillment?

(d) The role of chance in the processes of biological evolution has offended the sensibilities of some sufficiently to
lead to atheistic conclusions. It has also baffled many Christian theists. The position is that we have to recognize that
the process by which permanent changes (mutations) occur
in the material (DNA) carrying the genetic instructions to
succeeding generations of an organism is entirely random
with respect to its need for survival long enough to pro-
create — the condition for the survival of the species. Yet it
is the occurrence of such mutations which provides the
variation on which "natural selection" by the environment
favors some changes rather than others — and so produces
new species with the accumulation of change (sometimes
slowly, sometimes surprisingly rapidly). So "chance" seems
to be at work here, in both its sense of an event resulting
from so many multiple factors that we can only make statistical predictions of its outcome through our ignorance of
other than a few general factors (e.g., the symmetry of a
coin when tossed leading to a 50 percent chance of heads
or tails), and in the other sense of the intersection of two
independent causal chains. Both kinds of "chance" are involved in evolution: the former is exemplified in this context by the mutational event in the DNA, the latter by the

joint coincidence of mutational event and environmental situation, leading to a better-surviving form of the species. For Jacques Monod this meant that "pure chance, absolutely free but blind" lies "at the very root of the stupendous edifice of evolution,"[18] and from it he deduced the hopelessness of finding any meaning in the universe, in general, and in the human presence in it, in particular.

However, this randomness of molecular event in relation to biological consequence does not have to be raised to the level of a metaphysical principle interpreting the universe. For, in the behavior of matter on a larger scale many regularities, which have been raised to the level of being describable as "laws," arise from the combined effect of random microscopic events which constitute the macroscopic. So the involvement of chance at this level of mutation does not, of itself, preclude these events manifesting a law-like behavior at the level of populations of organisms.

Instead of being daunted by the role of chance in genetic mutations as being the manifestation of irrationality in the universe, it would be as consistent with the observations to assert that the full gamut of the potentialities of living matter could only be explored through the agency of the rapid and frequent randomization which is possible at the molecular level of the DNA. Indeed the role of chance is what one would expect if the universe were so constituted that all the potential forms of organization of matter (both living and non-living) which it contains might be explored. Moreover, even if the present biological world *is* only one out of an already large number of possibilities, the original primeval cloud of fundamental particles at the "hot big bang" must have had the *potentiality* of being able to develop into the complex molecular forms we call modern biological life. It is this that I find significant about the emergence of life in the universe; the role of chance is simply what is required if all the potentialities of the universe are going to be elicited effectively. So I see no objection to conceiving of God allowing the potentialities of his universe to be developed in all their ramifications through the operation of random events. It is as if chance is the search radar of God, sweeping through all the possible targets available to its probing — and these must be taken to include any "run" of possible universes that cosmologists have to postulate as having preceded our own. Chance can thus be seen as a creative agent, and we need not be daunted by the fact that the existence of life, and perhaps also of our actual universe, is the result of its operation. The fact is that matter-energy has in space-time, in *this* universe, acquired the ability to adopt self-replicating living structures which have acquired self-consciousness and the ability to *know* that they exist and how they evolved.

Since Monod made his contribution, there have been developments in theoretical biology which cast new light on the interrelation of chance and necessity in the origin and development of life. I refer to the investigations[19] of Prigogine and Eigen and their collaborators which now show how subtle can be the interplay of chance and necessity, of randomness and law, in the processes that led to the emergence of living structures. These studies demonstrate that the *mutual interplay of chance and law (necessity or determinism) is creative*, for it is the combination of the two which allows new forms to emerge and evolve.[20] Furthermore, the character of this interplay of chance and law appears now to be of a kind which makes it "inevitable" both that living structures should emerge and that they should evolve — given the physical and chemical properties of the atomic units (and presumably, therefore, of subatomic particles) in the universe we actually have. (According to these analyses, although the emergence of living systems may be "inevitable", it is nevertheless "indeterminate." For it is impossible to trace back the precise historical route or to predict the exact course of the future development, beyond certain time limits, because of the involvement of time-dependent random processes.) It now appears that the universe has potentialities which are becoming actualized by the joint operation in time of random, time-dependent processes in a framework of law-like properties — and that these potentialities include the possibility of biological, and so of human, life.

What can the assertion that there is a God who is Creator really mean in this new context? We need to rethink our models of God's action in the world. The potentialities of the stuff of this world, with their particular "given" properties, to elicit life (and so man) are written into creation by the Creator himself, and they are unveiled by chance exploring their gamut — a musical term meaning "the whole scale, range or compass of a thing" (O.E.D.). Perhaps I may be allowed to press the musical analogy further.

God as Creator we might now see as like a composer who, beginning with an arrangement of notes in an apparently simple tune, elaborates and expands it into a fugue by a variety of devices. Thus does a J. S. Bach create a complex and interlocking harmonious fusion of his original material. The listener to such a fugue experiences, with the luxuriant and profuse growth that emanates from the original simple structure, whole new worlds of emotional experience that are the result of the interplay between an expectation based on past experience ("law") and an openness to the new ("chance" in the sense that the listener cannot predict or control it). This is significant not only in the context of music itself — to those for whom music is an entering into communion with the mind of the composer (and even of God) — but also, in our present context, in its modelling of God's creative work for those to whom the whole world is sacramental. As in the enrichment that comes from the unfolding and elaboration of a celebration of the Christian Eucharist from a few simple acts and their associated words, so contemplation of creation as sacramental engenders experience of and possession by God who as the Holy Spirit moved, not only "on the face of the waters" at the beginning, but moves through it now transforming all into new forms, in and through the elaboration of the very stuff of the world.[21]

So might the Creator be imagined to unfold the potentialities of the universe which he himself has given it, selecting and shaping by his redemptive and providential action those that are to come to fruition — an Improvisor of unsurpassed ingenuity. One recalls in this connection that the music of creation has also been a constant theme of the religions of India, for example the South Indian representations, in bronze, of the dancing Shiva, the Creator-Destroyer, as Lord of the Dance of creation.

Both images, of the writing of a fugue and of the execution of a dance, serve to express the idea of God enjoying, of playing in, creation. This is not an idea new to Christian thought. The Greek fathers, so Harvey Cox argues, contended that the creation of the world was a form of play. "God did it they insisted out of freedom, not because he had to, spontaneously and not in obedience to some inexorable law of necessity."[22]

The creative role of chance operating upon the necessities which are themselves created has led us, then, to accept models of God's activity which express God's gratuitousness and joy in creation as a whole, and not in man alone. The created world is then seen as an expression of the overflow of the divine generosity.

III. THE HIERARCHY OF NATURAL SYSTEMS: MAN AS AGENT — GOD AS AGENT

In my first lecture, I referred to our scientific understanding of the world as that of a hierarchy of natural systems, each with its own science — and so language, concepts, and methods—appropriate to its elucidation and investigation. I argued then that some at least of the concepts applicable to higher levels are autonomous, i.e., not logically reducible to those applicable to levels lower in the scale of complexity, even though the "higher," i.e., more complex, systems contained processes involving lower level entities. For example, to be an antireductionist biologist, vis-à-vis physics and chemistry, is not to be a vitalist postulating additional entities that constitute the "life" of matter in its living forms. What is true about this interface is also true at interfaces higher up in the scale of complexity, including man. That the language describing mental events is irreducible to that of cerebral physiological events is a proposition widely supported by philosophers of many different views on the mind-brain relation. The mental activity of "consciousness" does not have to be predicated of some new entity, the "mind," but is an activity of matter which emerges when its units have evolved a particular kind of organized complexity. Apart from any philosophical analysis, the evidence for the intimate relation between mental activity and the physico-chemical state of the brain is, of course, enormously strong. But "*Are* mental events identical with neurophysiological events?" This question has been at the center of philosophical debates in recent decades, and from the stands, as it were, I note that many philosophers now accept that there is identity between mental states and brain states, but that they differ as to whether this is a contingent or a necessary identity, and they also differ on whether or not mental events could be predicted. It appears that even materialist views of the body-mind relation often incorporate what other views are often designed to ensure, namely, the ability of the human brain in the human body to be a self-conscious free agent. I see no reason why Christian theology could not accept a body-mind identitist position that is qualified with respect to the "anomaly" of mental events and to their nonreducibility to the physical (cf. D. Davidson[23]), and that allows the autonomy of man as a free agent, as a "self." For the sense of the self as an agent remains a given fact of our experience of ourselves in relation to our bodies and to the world.

In reflecting on *man as agent*, we encounter a lacuna in our thinking: how can the mental events, which seem to be identical with the neurophysiological events, include a sense of selfhood and of agency with respect to the very body which experiences it? I suggest that this problem of how the human sense of being an agent, of being a self, an "I," can be related to its action in the world of physical causality, is of the same ilk as the relation of God to the world. How can God act in a world in which every event is tied to every other by regularities which the sciences explain with increasing competence? How can I, experiencing myself mentally as an agent, initiate processes within the chain of physical events constituting my body, processes which themselves *are* my intended action? *I* am not another cause alongside my body but simply my body in reasoned and intended action. Nevertheless in my experience of self as agent, I transcend any particular action or group of actions. For any one physical action, e.g. raising my arm, can express many different intentions in various contexts. In my actions I am a transcendent causal agent expressing myself in and through the physical structure of my body.

Can we not similarly conceive of *God as agent* in the world? God's transcendence over the world in which he is immanent implies that he expresses his intentions within the causal nexus of the natural world. God's transcendence must, of course, be of a higher order than that of man's self over his body, since God transcends the whole world process, but this could still be consistent with the world being that realm of physical causality and regularity which the sciences show it to be — as consistent, that is, as is the mental character of the experience of being a human agent with the implementation of such an agent's intentions within the causal nexus of his physical body.

The notion of God's relation to the world as being at least analogous to the relation of the human mind to the human body (God:world :: mind:body) has a long history, but was earlier always based on dualist assumptions about man and on interventionist assumptions about God's action in the world. Our new understanding of natural hierarchies, of the irreducibility of at least some higher level concepts, and our new assessment of the relation between consciousness and the brain now transforms the context within which such a model is developed.

We note, moreover, that the *meaning* of an action by a human agent is not to be found by scientific analysis of the processes going on in the agent's body but by discovering his reasons and intentions. The model therefore suggests that, if God is to be regarded as, in some sense, the agent of the nexus of physical events, then we should look for the meaning of these events in *his* reasons and intentions, i.e., his purposes. According to this model, all the law-like processes in the physical world are expressions of his creative purposes. He is in all that goes on in nature and its processes — even if his purposes must be regarded as not always fully implemented in a world which has generated apparently free human agents within itself.

However much we may regard God as immanent in and expressing himself as agent through the world process, he is, ultimately, beyond all such describing and experiencing of him; he is the perpetual Creator of that process and never ceases to be such. So the transcendence of God who is immanent is of a higher order (or "power"? — in the mathematical sense) of transcendence than that of the human agent over his own actions. Perhaps one should say that in one aspect, or mode, of his being God is transcendent

Creator but in another aspect he is, by analogy to human agency, transcendence-in-immanence and in this mode he acts within persons, being immanent in the whole physical nexus. If we go on to say that this is eternally true of God's being then we here come very close to the formulations of classical trinitarian doctrine.

To use man-as-agent as a tentative model of God-as-agent seems therefore to be suggestive and fruitful. It should however be noted that it is only the *functional* activity of man as agent, and not an ontological basis in the kind of being that man is, that provides the model. What man actually does and how he actually relates to the world, far from making intelligible the relation of God to the world (the doctrine of creation, if you like), generates only enigma and paradox. For, in the light of the enormous potentiality of man for creative good and for degradation and evil, destructive both of himself and the rest of the created world, we may well ask: What does God think he was and is up to in evolving man, this "glory, jest and riddle of the world"?

At man, biological evolution passes a critical point, for *this* evolved creature can attempt to act independently of the intentions of the Creator. It follows that in evolving man God was taking a risk in giving him this hazardous, yet potentially creative, ability to be free. There must have been, as it were, a *cost* to God in his giving man this gift of the possibility of becoming more than his predecessors. In other words, God in creating man was acting with supreme magnanimity on behalf of the good of another existent — what in human life would be regarded as an expression of love. So, it is meaningful to say that God's acts of creation are an expression of "love," an outgoing of his inner being on behalf of another, albeit created, person. God the Creator is the One of whom the First Epistle of John[24] says bluntly, "God is love."

Is it not reasonable to go further and to conclude that the creative loving action which operates in the universe, eventually bringing forth man, is not incorrectly described as that of a *suffering* Creator? For risking love on behalf of another who remains free always entails suffering in the human experience of love. It is moreover consistent with the processes of creation through evolution themselves being characterized by eliciting new life through suffering, pain, and death. So our "model" of God as the personal agent of the creative process has to be amplified to include an awareness of him as the Creator who suffers in, with, and through his creation as it brings into existence new and hazardous possibilities — most of all those implicit in the creation of man, the self-determining person.

To summarize:

IV. OUR UNDERSTANDING OF GOD'S ACTION IN THE REAL WORLD
(in the light of the knowledge of it provided by the sciences)

From the continuity and creativity of the processes of the natural world we inferred that God's creative relation to the world must be conceived of as a continuous, sustaining, creative action within these natural processes. This is what we meant by saying that the Creator is *immanent* in his creation, and that is why we look for his "meanings" *within* the world of which we are part.

But the natural processes of the world have led to the emergence within it of human beings who possess a sense of transcendence over their environment which serves to sharpen the quest for One who makes intelligible the fact that there is anything at all — the One who is ultimate Being and who gives being to all else. So we continue to postulate God the Creator as *transcendent* over all matter-energy-space-time, over all-that-is.

However, the concept of God the Creator as both immanent and transcendent was not entirely satisfactory when
applied to One who is the Creator of that in which he is
immanent. Of outstanding historical importance, of course,
in relation to this problem are the "Logos" concept and that
of God as Spirit. However, these two traditional "models"
need supplementing today—in the light of the perspective
of our present scientific knowledge of the world—by such
models as that of *pan-en-theism*, whereby the world is regarded as being, as it were, "within" God, but the being of
God is regarded as not exhausted by, or subsumed within,
the world. In this connection, a feminine image of God as
Creator proves to be a useful corrective to purely masculine
images by its ability to model God as creating a self-creative
world *within* God's own Being.

We would also have to say, as a consequence of the created order being continuously God in action, that although
God is not more present at one time or place than at others
(he is not a substance, all is of God at all times), nevertheless we find that in some sequences of events in created
nature and history God unveils his meaning to us more than
in others. There are *meanings* of God to be unveiled, but
not all are read: some events will be more revealing than
others. Moreover, any meanings unveiled in the *various and
distinctive levels* of the world must be complementary, and
not all have pertinence in the human search for meaning
and intelligibility.

We have found that the processes of the world are *open-
ended* and that there are *emergent* in space-time new organizations of matter-energy which often require epistemologi-
cally *nonreducible* language to expound their distinctiveness.
Thus it was that I ventured the idea of God as "exploring"
in creation, of actualizing all the potentialities of his creation, of improvising and of unfolding fugally all the deriva-
tions and combinations inherently possible. The meanings

of God unveiled to and for *man* will be the more partial, broken, and incomplete the more the level of creation being examined departs from the human and personal, in which the transcendence of the "I" is experienced as immanent in our bodies. The more personal and *self*-conscious is the entity in which God is immanent, the more capable is it of expressing God's supra-*personal* characteristics.

This stress on emergence is one-sided without a balancing emphasis on the *continuity* that is required by the scientific perception of natural processes. Any new meaning which God is able to express in a new emergent should thus not be discontinuous with the meanings expressed in that out of which it has emerged. So it is that the transcendence-in-immanence of human experience raises the hope and conjecture that in *a* human person adequate for the purpose, immanence might be able to display in a uniquely emergent mode a transcendent dimension to a degree that could *unveil*, without distortion, the transcendent *Creator*—which is what is meant by "incarnation."

Furthermore, from a consideration of the character of the natural processes of suffering and death and from a recognition that God has put his own purposes at risk in creating free, self-conscious persons, we have tentatively recognized that *God suffers with Creation and in the creative process*—that is, God *is* Love.

And so our two paths to reality of science and religion begin to converge as each points to a depth of reality beyond the power of model or metaphor, in which all that is created is embraced in the inner unity of the divine life of the Creator—transcendent, incarnate, and immanent. We can but echo Dante in his ultimate vision of the divine unity:

> Thither my own wings could not carry me,
>   But that a flash my understanding clove
>   Whence its desire came to it suddenly.

High phantasy lost power and here broke off;
    Yet, as a wheel moves smoothly, free from jars,
    My will and my desire were turned by love,

The love that moves the sun and the other stars.

[*Paradiso*, end of Canto XXXIII[25]]

The rest is silence.

Notes

1. WAYS TO THE REAL WORLD

1. Alexsandr Solzhenitsyn, "Templeton Award Address," 10 May 1983 (Grand Cayman, B.W.I.: Lismore Press, 1983; and London *Times*, 11 May 1983).

2. Cf. J. W. Draper, *History of the Conflict between Religion and Science* (London: King, 1875); A. D. White, *A History of the Warfare of Science with Theology in Christendom* (New York: Appleton, 1896); J. Y. Simpson, *Landmarks in the Struggle between Science and Religion* (London: Hodder & Stoughton, 1925).

3. Q.v., John Passmore, *Science and Its Critics* (London: Duckworth, 1978).

4. I refer *inter alia* to the broad spectrum of views, including positivism and instrumentalism, of such authors as Carnap, Hempel, Nagel, and Braithwaite.

5. See the comprehensive account of F. Suppe, *The Structure of Scientific Theories*, 2nd ed. (Urbana: University of Illinois Press, 1977).

6. Mary Hesse, *Revolutions and Reconstructions in the Philosophy of Science* (Brighton: Harvester Press, 1981), xii.

7. The argument of Duhem, Poincaré, Einstein, and Quine. See A. Grunbaum, "The Duhemian Argument," *Phil. Sci.* 27 (1): 75-87, for summary and discussion.

8. The ideas of Bohm, Feyerabend, Hanson, Kuhn, Hesse, and Toulmin.

9. Following the pioneer work of R. K. Merton in the 1930s.

10. M. Mulkay, *Science and the Sociology of Knowledge* (London: Allen & Unwin, 1979), 59-60.

11. D. Bloor, *Knowledge and Social Imagery* (London: Routledge & Kegan Paul, 1976), 4, 5.

12. Mulkay, 60-62.

13. E. McMullin, in *The Sciences and Theology in the Twentieth Century*, ed. A. R. Peacocke (Notre Dame: University of Notre Dame Press, 1981, and Stocksfield and London: Oriel Press, 1981), 301-02.

14. Here by "testing" McMullin refers not so much to short-term prediction but rather to the guidance of theory into fruitful pathways of extension and modification. Such a testing process operating over the years separates out what is truth-bearing.

15. W. H. Newton-Smith, *The Rationality of Science* (London: Routledge & Kegan Paul, 1981), 259.

16. Ibid., 264.

17. Suppe, *The Structure of Scientific Theories*.

18. H. W. Putnam, *Mathematics, Matter and Method*, Vol. 1 (Cambridge: Cambridge University Press, 1975), 69ff.

19. W. Sellars, *Science, Perception and Reality* (New York: Humanities Press, 1962; London: Routledge & Kegan Paul, 1963), 97n.

20. B. C. van Fraasen, *The Scientific Image* (Oxford: Clarendon Press, 1980), 8.

21. It is somewhat unfortunate, because easily confused with a naive interpretation, that van Fraasen uses the word "literally" in his statement. He supports this by saying it is meant to exclude conventionalism, logical positivism, and instrumentalism since it indicates that the statements of science really are *capable* of being true and false and that, if a scientific theory says something exists, this implication cannot be removed in any construal of it (as *The Scientific Image*, 10, 11). Even so, in the context of the present discussion — when "literal" might be likened to "literal," naive fundamentalist interpretation of, say, the biblical literature — the presence of this word in von Fraasen's statement is, to say the least, unfortunate. For it does not do justice to the range of degrees of acceptance of the scientific theories that are actually put forward in relation to the very different kinds of subject matter that constitute science at a particular time.

22. E. McMullin, "The Case for Scientific Realism," in *Essays on Scientific Realism*, ed. J. Leplin (Berkeley: University of California Press, 1984).

23. A. R. Peacocke, *Creation and the World of Science* (Oxford: Clarendon Press, 1979), 21-22.

24. A phrase of R. M. Harré, e.g., in *Theories and Things* (London and New York: Sheed & Ward, 1961).

25. Peacocke, *Creation and the World of Science*, 21-22.

26. Ian Hacking, *Representing and Intervening* (Cambridge: Cambridge University Press, 1983), especially Chapter 16, "Experimentation and scientific realism."

27. Ibid., 262-265.

28. Ibid., 275.

29. J. Worrall (*Phil. Quart.* 32 [1982]: 201-31) describes "conjec-

tural realism," based on K. Popper, in the following terms: "our theories are attempts truly to describe the structure of the universe. . . . Theories are true-or-false attempted descriptions of reality, both observable and 'hidden'. Our present best guide . . . to the structure of the reality hidden behind the phenomena is the guide supplied by our presently best theories. But a different theory, one which gives a quite new account of 'hidden reality', may become 'presently best' tomorrow . . . we cannot have any guarantee that our present highest level picture of reality will be preserved, even approximately, in the new theory. . . . The best we can say is that our present theory in a given field yields our best guess about the truth in that field — that may well be wrong nonetheless" (229-30).

30. Peacocke, *Creation and the World of Science*, 21-22.

31. I. Barbour, *Issues in Science and Religion* (1966; repr. New York: Harper Torch books, 1971).

32. Ian T. Ramsey, *Models and Mystery* (Oxford: Oxford University Press, 1964); *Models for Divine Activity* (London: S.C.M. Press, 1973).

33. Q.v., *inter alia* S. McFague, *Metaphorical Theology* (London: S.C.M. Press, and Philadelphia: Fortress Press, 1983), and Barbour, *Issues in Science and Religion*.

34. Janet M. Soskice, "The Use of Metaphor as a Conceptual Vehicle in Religious Language," D.Phil. thesis, University of Oxford, 1982. (To be published as *Metaphor and Religious Language*, Oxford: Oxford University Press, 1984). I am greatly indebted to Dr. Soskice for making her thesis available to me. As I hope my references show I have been greatly impressed by her argument, only an outline of which I had myself previously partly developed (in *Creation and the World of Science*, 21-22).

35. Ibid., 159.

36. Barbour, *Issues in Science and Religion*, 158.

37. For further discussion, see I. Barbour, *Myths, Models and Paradigms* (London: S.C.M. Press, 1974), especially pp. 42-43; F. Ferré, "Metaphors, Models and Religion", *Soundings* 2 (1968): 334.

38. Soskice, 88.

39. Such ("theory-constitutive") metaphors that propose a model should, according to Janet Soskice's careful analysis, be distinguished from "metaphorical terms" (or "metaphorically constituted theory terms") which are the linguistic projections of such a model (e.g., "feedback," etc. in the example in the text). It is these latter which are at the center of the debate about reality-depiction in the philosophy of science (Soskice, 161-62).

40. W. V. Quine, "A Postscript on Metaphor," in *On Metaphors*,

ed. S. Sacks (Chicago: University of Chicago Press, 1979), 159.

41. Cf. Ramsey, *Models and Mystery*, 13; F. Ferré, *Basic Modern Philosophy of Religion* (London: Allen & Unwin, 1968), 375.

42. N. R. Campbell, "The Structure of Theories," in *Readings in the Philosophy of Science*, ed. H. Feigl and M. Brodbeck (New York: Appleton-Century-Crofts, 1953) 297-98.

43. Soskice, 181-82

44. E. McMullin ("The Case for Scientific Realism") cites a geological example, namely the way in which the model of continental drift developed, by evoking anomalies and new evidence, into the plate-tectonic model. This feature of good models supports the realist position, McMullin argues, because such fertile developments of a model are best explained by supposing "that the model approximates sufficiently well to the structures of the world which are causally responsible for the phenomena to be explained to make it profitable for the scientist to take its metaphoric extensions seriously. . . . The antirealist cannot . . . make sense of such sequences which are pretty numerous in the recent history of all the natural sciences. . . ." "Science aims at fruitful metaphor and at ever more detailed structure . . . the resources of metaphor are essential to the work of science, and the construction and retention of metaphor must be seen as part of the aim of science."

45. Following McFague, *Metaphorical Theology*, and Barbour, *Myths, Models and Paradigms*.

46. E.g., according to S. McFague, I. Barbour, F. Ferré, N. P. Hanson, R. Harré, M. Hesse (in her earlier works).

47. The theories of reference in question being the "causal" ones typically developed by S. Kripke, H. W. Putnam, and K. Donellan, and the "experimentational" one of I. Hacking (*Representing and Intervening*).

48. Soskice, 196ff.

49. Ibid., 210-11.

50. Whether the reference was made ("baptismally") by ostension with historical chains of usage, or, for physical magnitudes, by "dubbing" x as "x is whatever caused (and could still, in a repeat experiment, cause) this state of affairs" — say a galvanometer needle to jump if x is "electricity."

51. F. J. Ayala, in the Introduction to *Studies in the Philosophy of Biology*, ed. F. J. Ayala and T. Dobzhansky (London: Macmillan, 1974).

52. For a fuller discussion of the subject of this section (reduction-

ism, etc.) see A. R. Peacocke, "Reductionism: A Review of the Epistemological Issues and their Relevance to Biology and the Problem of Consciousness," *Zygon* 11 (1976): 306-34.

53. Many of these concepts (though not all — it is a matter for investigation in each instance) turn out to be *sui generis*, characteristic and specific to that level, e.g., many biological concepts vis-à-vis physics-and-chemistry (genetic information transfer in relation to polynucleotide chemistry), many social relationships in relation to individual psychology or to genetics, etc.

54. In its widest sense, including all the facets of the practice of religion — worship, prayer, ritual, sacrament, meditation, contemplation, rites of passage, etc. For a report on the work of the R.E.R.U., see Sir Alister Hardy, *The Spiritual Nature of Man* (Oxford: Clarendon Press, 1979).

55. R. W. Hepburn, "Demythologising and the Problem of Validity," in *New Essays in Philosophical Theology*, ed. A. Flew and A. MacIntyre, (London: S.C.M. Press, 1955), 237.

56. Barbour, *Myths, Models and Paradigms*, 34-38.

57. McFague, *Metaphorical Theology*, 132-33.

58. Cf. R. B. Braithwaite, "An Empiricist's View of the Nature of Religious Belief," repr. in *Christian Ethics and Contemporary Philosophy*, ed. I. T. Ramsey (London: S.C.M. Press, 1956).

59. Ramsey, *Models and Mystery, Models for Divine Activity*, and *Religious Language* (London: S.C.M. Press, 1957).

60. E.g., Barbour, *Myths, Models and Paradigms*, 34-38; F. Ferré, *Basic Modern Philosophy of Religion*; D. Tracy, "Metaphor and Religion," in *On Metaphor*, ed. S. Sacks (Chicago: University of Chicago Press, 1979); T. Fawcett, *The Symbolic Language of Religion* (London: S.C.M. Press, 1970); S. McFague, *Metaphorical Theology*; and Soskice.

61. J. Macquarrie, "God and the World," *Theology* 25 (1972): 394-403.

62. Cf. the exposition in A. R. Peacocke, *Science and the Christian Experiment* (London: Oxford University Press, 1971), 12-28.

63. McFague, 104

64. Fawcett, 82.

65. Soskice, 167.

66. Ibid., 176.

67. Ibid., 217.

68. Report of the Doctrine Commission of the Church of England, *Christian Believing* (London: S.P.C.K., 1976), 1.

69. Soskice, 216. The word "cause" here in her formulation is am-

biguous since God is not a "cause" in the sense of a scientifically describable cause within the nexus of events that constitute the natural
order. God is that which gives being to all-that-is, and so, in this sense,
is a cosmos-explaining-being; he is that which renders all-that-is intelligible. So the word "cause" has to be taken in this qualified sense when
predicated of God as Creator. This must be so understood in any use
of the designation "God is that which is the source and 'cause' of all
there is."

70. McFague, 134, quoting P. Ricoeur, *The Rule of Metaphor*, trans.
R. Czerny (Toronto: University of Toronto Press, 1977), 243-46.

71. Loren Eiseley, *The Star Thrower* (London: Wildwood House,
1978), 120-21.

2. GOD'S ACTION IN THE REAL WORLD

1. This second lecture is largely a re-presentation of material to be
found in the author's *Creation and the World of Science* with a view to
illustrating how the dialogue between the scientific and theological
enterprises might be conducted in regard to one particular problem —
that of finding intelligible and plausible models for depicting the reality
of God's relation to the world, now understood in terms of the natural
sciences.

2. K. Heim, *The Transformation of the Scientific World-view* (London: S.C.M. Press, 1953), 24.

3. K. Denbigh, *An Inventive Universe* (London: Hutchinson, 1975),
156.

4. H. K. Schilling, *The New Consciousness in Science and Religion*
(London: S.C.M. Press, 1973), 126.

5. Isaac Newton, *Principia*, Scholicum to Definition VIII, 1; re-
printed in H. G. Alexander, *The Leibniz-Clarke Correspondence* (Manchester: Manchester University Press, 1956, 1965), 152.

6. J. Polkinghorne, *The Particle Play* (Oxford and San Francisco:
W. H. Freeman, 1979), 125.

7. Sir Bernard Lovell, "In the Centre of Immensities," *Advance-
ment of Science*, N.S. 1 (1975): 6.

8. Q.v., B. Carter, "Large Number Coincidences and the Anthropic Principle in Cosmology," in *Confrontation of Cosmological
Theories with Observations Data*, ed. M. S. Longair (I.A.U., 1974),
291-98; B. J. Carr and M. J. Rees, *Nature (Lond.)* 278 (1979): 605-12;
G. Gale, *Sci. Amer.* 245 (1981): 114-122.

9. Lovell, 6.

10. C. W. Misner, K. S. Thorne, and J. A. Wheeler, *Gravitation* (San Francisco: W. H. Freeman, 1973), Ch. 44.

11. "Who is this that darkeneth counsel by words without knowledge? Gird up thy loins like a man; for I will demand of thee, and answer thou me. Where wast thou when I laid the foundations of the earth? Declare, if thou hast understanding" (Job. 38 v.1-4, A.V.).

12. St. Augustine, *Confessions*, ch. 11, paras. 14, 30; trans. R. S. Pinecoffin (Harmondsworth: Penguin Classics, 1961) 263, 279.

13. J.-P. Caussade, *The Sacrament of the Present Moment*, trans. K. Muggeridge (London: Collins, 1981).

14. *Oxford Dictionary of the Christian Church*, 1st ed., ed. F. L. Cross (London: Oxford University Press, 1970), 1010.

15. T. Dobzhansky, *The Biology of Ultimate Concern* (New York: New American Library, 1967), 129.

16. F. Jacob, *The Logic of Living Systems* (London: Allen Lane, 1974), 13.

17. G. G. Simpson, *The Meaning of Evolution* (New Haven: Yale University Press, 1971), 201.

18. J. Monod, *Chance and Necessity* (London: Collins, 1972), 110.

19. For a fuller exposition of the scientific principles see A. R. Peacocke, *An Introduction to the Physical Chemistry of Biological Organization* (Oxford: Clarendon Press, 1983), especially chapters 2 and 5.

20. As beautifully exemplified, with reference to many contexts, in M. Eigen and R. Winkler, *Das Spiel* (Munich and Zurich: R. Piper, 1975); English translation, *The Laws of the Game*, trans. R. and R. Kimber (New York: Knopf, 1981, and London: Allen Lane, 1982).

21. I am indebted to Dr. Jean van Altena for this illuminating extension of the fugal image to the Christian Eucharist and for other phrases in these paragraphs.

22. Harvey Cox, *The Feast of Fools* (Cambridge: Harvard University Press, 1969), 151.

23. D. Davidson, "Mental events," in *Experience and Theory*, ed. L. Foster and J. W. Swanson (Amherst: University of Massachusetts Press, 1970).

24. I John 4: 9, 16.

25. Dante, *Paradiso*, end of Canto XXXIII (from the translation by Barbara Reynolds [London: Penguin Books, 1962]).

Index